AND EDUCATION

Literacy and Education tells the story of how literacy—starting in the early 1980s—came to be seen not as a mental phe-

ssible
hows
o the
eracy
rning
ludes
lened
itexts
ogies.

sor of
uthor
course

Analysis, fourth edition, *Language and Learning in the Digital Age* and is co-editor of *The Routledge Handbook of Discourse Analysis*.

Routledge Key Ideas in Education Series

Series Editors: Greg Dimitriadis and Bob Lingard

LITERACY
AND EDUCATION

JAMES PAUL GEE

Routledge
Taylor & Francis Group
NEW YORK AND LONDON

First published 2015
by Routledge
711 Third Avenue, New York, NY 10017

Simultaneously published in the UK
by Routledge
2 Park Square, Milton Park, Abingdon, Oxon OX14 4RN

Routledge is an imprint of the Taylor & Francis Group, an informa business

Library of Congress Cataloging-in-Publication Data
Gee, James Paul.
   Literacy and education / James Paul Gee.
      pages cm. — (Routledge key ideas in education)
   Includes bibliographical references and index.
   1. Literacy.   2. Literacy—Social aspects.   3. Digital media—Social aspects.
4. Education.   I. Title.
   LC149.G44 2015
   302.2'244—dc23
   2014026450

ISBN: 978-1-138-82602-1 (hbk)
ISBN: 978-1-138-82604-5 (pbk)
ISBN: 978-1-315-73957-1 (ebk)

Typeset in Minion
by Apex CoVantage, LLC

To Bead

CONTENTS

SERIES EDITORS' INTRODUCTION

This series introduces key people and topics and discusses their particular implications for the field of education. Written by the most prominent thinkers in the field, these "key ideas" are read through the series' authors' past and present work, with particular attention given to the ways these ideas can, do, and might impact theory, research, practice, and policy in education.

More specifically, these texts offer particular conversations with prominent authors, whose work has resonated across education and related fields. Books in this series read as conversations with authorities, whose thinking has helped constitute these ideas and their role in the field of education—yesterday, today, and tomorrow.

Much more than introductions alone, these short, virtuosic volumes look to shape ongoing discussions in the field of education by putting the field's contemporary luminaries in dialogue with its foundational figures and critical topics. From new students to senior scholars, these volumes will spark the imaginations of a range of readers thinking through key ideas and education.

PREFACE

This is a book about literacy as more than the mental ability to write and read. The book argues that literacy is social because the mind itself is social.

This is also a book about the connections among literacy, oral language, learning, technology, human experience, and social forces as they all work together. Literacy is inseparable from its "playmates." It needs to be studied that way, not in isolation.

This book is, for me, a retrospective work in that it brings together ideas that I have developed over a long time. Does this mean the book is about me? No, because any talk about "my ideas" is shorthand for all those fellow scholars with whom I worked and played. Our ideas infected each other like viruses. And, for all of us our viruses were caught from others earlier on the scene, before we ourselves mutated them and passed them on. In turn, we hope that our viruses will be mutated and transformed by others who come later.

This book is but one perspective on literacy. It is a perspective located in but one patch of a much larger field ("language and literacy"). While I certainly think some patches of the larger field are barren, I also think many others bear tasty fruit and merit a visit with some other guide.

From the perspective of this book, literacy is not a minor or isolated topic. In fact, it is too big for one discipline. It must be studied by a team effort equipped with different disciplines, skills, insights, and methods. The team does not always have to see eye-to-eye, but they are in the same boat together.

The book deals with schools—and competing forms of literacy and learning outside of school—because in societies like ours we see school as literacy's most cherished home. We have great expectations for schools and for the types of literacy they sponsor. Unfortunately, too often our expectations are dashed. And, further, today schools face a myriad of challenges in the name of "21st century skills" fit for our modern, high-risk, high-tech global world, skills that are not on offer in too many of our schools.

Our modern world cannot but help to be a background in any book about literacy as an active force in the world. We live in a world with massive inequality and facing many serious dangers from complex interacting systems like the environment, global warming, the global economy, civilizational and religious conflicts, broken politics, and high-tech forms of surveillance and warfare. I do not discuss my political views on these serious issues in this book much (see my book *The Anti-Education Era*, New York: Palgrave/Macmillan, 2013). Rather, I argue that the perspective this book takes on literacy is one important prerequisite for thinking about, coping with, and changing our imperiled world.

The first chapter is background, overview, and motivation for continuing. The second chapter is about literacy. The third is about literacy's close companions: the mind, the body, human experience, and learning. The final chapter is about digital media and new forms of learning they have helped to inspire, two of literacy's newer companions.

At times, this book reprises, revises, and recombines ideas from a number of past books of mine that in each case offer more detail and further references. These books are:

Social Linguistics and Literacies. London: Routledge. First Edition, 1990. Fifth Edition, 2015.

The Social Mind. New York: Bergin & Garvey. 1992. Reprinted Edition: Champaign-Urbana: Common Ground

An Introduction to Discourse Analysis. London: Routledge. 1999. Fourth Edition, 2014.

How to Do Discourse Analysis. London: Routledge. 2010. Second Edition, 2014.

Situated Language and Learning. London: Routledge. 2004.

What Video Games Have to Teach Us About Learning and Literacy. New York: Palgrave/Macmillan. 2003. Second Edition, 2007.

Good Video Games and Good Learning. New York: Peter Lang. 2007. Second Edition, 2013.

Women as Gamers (with Elisabeth Hayes). New York: Palgrave/Macmillan. 2010.

Language and Learning in the Digital Age (with Elisabeth Hayes). London: Routledge. 2011.

Collected Essays on Learning and Assessment in the Digital Age. Champaign-Urbana: Common Ground. 2014.

A note, then, before we begin: I did not want to clutter a short book like this with references. The literature on literacy, even on literacy from a sociocultural perspective, is vast. To cite any significant part of that literature would render the text unreadable and too long. So, I cite major accessible sources. Readers can follow up through these to gain many more things to read and ponder. The books cited above have ample bibliographies as well.

1

INTRODUCTION

A Story

Let me start with a story. I began my academic career forty years ago as a linguist studying the structure of language ("grammar"). At that time, thanks to the seminal work of Noam Chomsky, the fashionable thing to study was the basic design properties of language, the core grammatical properties that all human languages shared (Chomsky 1957, 1986). There was much less interest in meaning and in language in use. The study of language was then a pretty abstract affair.

Thanks to the "accidents" of life—mistakes made, lessons learned—years later I found myself employed in an applied linguistics program. The program happened to be in a School of Education. I knew absolutely nothing about education then. Early in my time there the Dean of the School of Education came up to me and asked me to attend a meeting about applying for a grant to research adult literacy.

As a generative (Chomskian) linguist I believed that only oral language was real language. Literacy was only a derivative and relatively trivial "code." After all, oral language arose in humans long ago (Pinker 1994). It is a good part of what separated humans from their primate relatives. On the other hand, literacy is a relatively recent cultural invention (Olson 1996). Writing has been invented independently only a few times in history. All human groups have had oral language, but not all cultures have had literacy and not all have it today. In the not too distant past, in fact, literacy was rare within societies and across the world.

When I attended the meeting, I was surprised to find out there were any adults in the United States who were "illiterate," let alone the supposed millions I was told were so or close to it. Since everyone in the U.S. went to school, how could this have happened? I assumed schools gave everyone an equal chance and at least ensured that everyone learned to read and write.

When I attended the meeting, I was as naïve as I could be. I thought that surely literacy would be a simple, straightforward topic of little depth (I should have known better, since many languages in the world do not even have a word for "literacy"). Surely, literacy was just a practical matter of no theoretical interest. It was not something real academics would study.

As I studied literacy the whole topic seemed stranger and stranger. Simplicity turned to complexity. Paradoxes abounded.

The Story Continues

Because I had been "coerced" to work on literacy and was trying to get any help I could, I ended up meeting Sarah Michaels,
then working at Harvard and now at Clark University. My colleague David Dickinson (now at Vanderbilt) introduced me
to Sarah.

Sarah showed me data she and others had collected on
first-grade "sharing-time" sessions in schools. Sharing time
is something teachers of very young children tend to do to
start off the school day. It is sometimes called "rug time" or
"show and tell." At the time I could not have imagined anything seemingly less important.

Sarah and her colleagues had found that some African-
American children gave sharing-time turns that were different
from those of the white children in the classrooms (Cazden
2001; Michaels 1981; Michaels & Cazden 1986; Michaels &
Cook-Gumperz 1979; Michaels & Collins 1984). These African-
American children told what Sarah called "topic-associating"
stories, while the Anglo children (and some of the other African-
American children) told "topic-centered" stories.

Topic-associating stories were ones that appeared to move
from topic to topic with no overt theme. The unifying theme
had to be supplied by the listener. Topic-centered stories were
ones that focused on and developed one unitary explicit topic.
These were usually, in fact, not really stories but reports, such
as an "event cast" of a trip to a swimming pool, or procedures,
such as the steps involved in making a candle.

The African-American children's sharing-time turns were
not well received by their teachers. The teachers thought the
children were rambling on and not making sense. The teachers

in these classrooms had instituted a rule that each turn had to be about "one important thing" and felt the African-American children often violated this rule.

The teachers, it turns out, could seamlessly interrupt and interact with the white children and the African-American children who told topic-focused stories, though not with the topic-associating African-American children. In a sort of interactive dance the teachers helped the topic-focused children produce a piece of language that, while spoken, was explicit and topic-focused in the way we later expect school-based writing to be.

Sarah and her colleagues argued that these sharing-time sessions were early practice at literacy or literate language for children who could not yet read and write very well. This was not necessarily the teachers' conscious plan, but it seemed to be the underlying goal in their practice.

When I looked at the sharing-time data, a number of the African-American stories stood out. They were long, robust, well-organized poetic stories. Unfortunately, the researchers had thrown these stories out of their data, concentrating on the shorter ones told by the African-American children. They did this in order "control for length," since the white children's sharing-time turns, in particular, were relatively short (because they were so concise).

It appeared to me that some of the shorter African-American turns were cases where children had been stopped by the teacher and told to sit down (for not talking about one important thing). Or they were cases where the child had started a story, but for one reason or another did not choose to finish it. The stories that were clearly finished seemed thematically based, but not loosely structured. While they were not like early versions of the sort of explicit, concise language we later expect in reports and essays, they were "literate" in the sense of being early versions of the literary language we expect in poetry and other forms of literary art.

Let me give you an example. Below I reprint one of these stories that I have used a number of times in my writings (e.g., Gee 1985). This is a story by a girl the researchers called "Leona," a little girl about whom a good deal has come to be written by different people over the years:

THE PUPPY STORY

I. SETTING

STANZA 1

1. Last yesterday in the morning
2. there was a hook on the top of the stairway
3. an' my father was pickin' me up
4. an I got stuck on the hook up there

STANZA 2

5. an' I hadn't had breakfast
6. he wouldn't take me down
7. until I finished all my breakfast
8. cause I didn't like oatmeal either

II. CATALYST

STANZA 3

9. an' then my puppy came
10. he was asleep
11. he tried to get up
12. an' he ripped my pants
13. an' he dropped the oatmeal all over him

STANZA 4

14. an' my father came
15. an' he said "did you eat all the oatmeal?"
16. he said "where's the bowl?"
17. I said "I think the dog took it"
18. "Well I think I'll have t'make another bowl"

III. CRISIS

STANZA 5

19. an' so I didn't leave till seven
20. an' I took the bus
21. an' my puppy he always be following me
22. my father said "he—you can't go"

STANZA 6

23. an' he followed me all the way to the bus stop
24. an' I hadda go all the way back
25. by that time it was seven thirty
26. an' then he kept followin' me back and forth
27. an' I hadda keep comin' back

IV. EVALUATION

STANZA 7

28. an' he always be followin' me
29. when I go anywhere
30. he wants to go to the store
31. an' only he could not go to places where we could go
32. like to the stores he could go
33. but he have to be chained up

V. RESOLUTION

STANZA 8

34. an' we took him to the emergency
35. an' see what was wrong with him
36. an' he got a shot
37. an' then he was crying

STANZA 9

38. an' last yesterday, an' now they put him asleep
39. an' he's still in the hospital
40. an' the doctor said he got a shot because
41. he was nervous about my home that I had

VI. CODA

STANZA 10

42. an' he could still stay but
43. he thought he wasn't gonna be able to let him go.

Thanks to those vagaries of life I mentioned earlier, I had done some work on "oral literature." To anyone at the time familiar with the literature on oral literature (Bauman & Sherzer 1974; Finnegan 1967, 1977; Hymes 1981; Tedlock 1983), Leona's story was a quite recognizable linguistic event.

Leona used aspects of the even then well-studied dialect of African-American Vernacular English (Baugh 1983, 1999; Labov 1972; Smitherman 1977). For example, the "naked be" in "My puppy he always be followin' me" in line 21 (repeated in line 28): In Leona's dialect this is a habitual/durative aspect marker. Here it means that the puppy habitually, as a matter of habit, as part of the puppy's inherent way of acting, continually seeks to follow her (and thereby creates problems and eventually an opposition to the adult discipline of the home).

Leona uses poetic devices that are the hallmark of oral literature across the world (devices apparent in adult form in Homer and the Bible, which started as oral stories, see Finnegan 1977; Foley 1988; Havelock 1976; Hymes 1981; Ong 1982; Pattison 1982; Tedlock 1983). These devices include repetition, stylistic variation, and syntactic and semantic parallelism, all of which are readily apparent in Leona's stories. By the way, saying that someone is in an "oral culture" does not mean that they and other members of their culture are not literate. It means only that their culture retains a strong allegiance to thematically based, culturally significant face-to-face storytelling.

For example, notice how in Stanzas 3 and 4 Leona introduces the puppy and the father in parallel ways, first opening Stanza 3 with "my puppy came" and then opening Stanza 4 with "my father came". Leona then attaches four events to each of these entrances; she assigns four acts to the puppy and four pieces of dialogue to the father. This is one of many devices that create an opposition between the youthful puppy that wants to go free and the adult world that wants discipline.

Leona uses a device characteristic of African-American storytelling (and the storytelling of some other cultures). She uses non-narrative material to key the listener into what the "point" or basic theme of her story is. In her case (in this and others of her stories) she does this by exiting the main story line just before her story is about to end and giving the listener some non-narrative information. This non-narrative information is the sort of information Labov called "evaluation," namely, material that signals what makes the story tellable or what its point is (Labov 1972; Labov & Waletsky 1967).

Thus, in Stanza 7 we are not given story events (this happened, then this happened), but generalizations (e.g., note, too, the repetition of the habitual/durative "be" and the repetition of "go"). This stanza clearly tells us—which the habitual/durative marker has already signaled—that the theme of the story is the conflict between the puppy (and Leona as a child?) continually wanting to go free and having, by adult dictate, to be chained up (unfree) [recall the hook earlier in the story]. It is this conflict that must be resolved for the story to be resolved and it is resolved in the last stanzas when an adult authority figure (the doctor) dictates that the puppy cannot "go" (free). [In more adult narratives, evaluation material is often spread out throughout the story, though Leona, as other young children, tended to concentrate it right before her conclusion.]

The teacher worried about whether or not the puppy was dead (put to sleep), where exactly the puppy was now, and over exactly how much time these events took place. But these concerns are beside the point in such oral-literature stories. Such stories exist primarily to carry themes and develop themes, themes of importance to their tellers and their cultures. They are meant to be exaggerated in ways that bring home those themes (e.g., the hook in the beginning of the story). Leona's theme here—that young things have to follow adult rules (here represented by parents, schools, and doctors) as part and parcel of growing up—is a primordial theme for children and adults in many cultures.

So Leona has given the teacher a quite recognizable linguistic performance ("oral literature"). Her performance was rooted in a long history of African-Americans going back to Africa. It is a type of performance once prevalent in many other cultures, though done in somewhat different ways in each. It is also a type of performance that, via figures like

Homer and Chaucer, is the foundation of Western written literature. Of course, Leona was a young child and, thus, early in her apprenticeship to this cultural verbal style, though obviously well on her way.

One thing that went on in classrooms like the one Leona was in was that children like her were misled by the ways in which teachers (and many academics) use the word "story" to cover both narrative verbal texts with plots and oral texts more akin to reports or the news (e.g., going swimming or making candles). In fact, following the original sharing-time terminology I have continued this unfortunate tradition here.

Leona thinks the teacher really wants a story and gives her a culturally embedded version of one. But the teacher is actually after a news-like report through which she can scaffold early school-based literate language in the "expository" style (i.e., linear, sequenced, concise, explicit, non-poetic, non-literary, expository language). All children need practice in many different styles, of course. But such a lack of clarity about goals, practice, and what language means creates a fundamental unfairness.

Leona and what she is doing are being misrecognized. She is being seen as deficient when she is enacting a culturally known, important, and impressive way of being, making meaning, and using language. She is not being seen as an African-American storyteller. Furthermore, she is not being helped to recognize the ways with words the teacher expects. The teacher assumes she already knows what is wanted—what the "rules of the game" are—and does not tell her. Many of the "mainstream" children (white and black) in the classrooms had engaged in sharing-time-like reports to their parents at dinner time, another now well-studied phenomenon.

A deep problem here is that Leona is a very young girl. She is being told by an authority figure, as part of her early socialization into schooling, that she does not make sense. This is not because the teacher is a bad person. It is because she does not know that Leona is using ways with words that have come from her early socialization into her own home culture, a culture tied to the historical legacy of oral literature. This "cultural misunderstanding" (misrecognition, missed opportunities for recognition) can and often does alienate children like Leona from school and school-based language and literacy. It can force such young children to choose between family and school in terms of who makes sense.

Literacy

I was confronted with the sharing-time data at the same time my Dean was pushing me to work on literacy. It was a time, as I mentioned before, when I knew nothing about education and had never stepped foot in a public school. I had been a product of Catholic schools. Though I had not been in one, I assumed that public schools were all about leveling the playing field. Confronted with the sharing-time data, my first thought was: Here is a deep *theoretical* problem, not just a deep practical and ethical problem (Gee 2011).

How could a child bring a language practice to school that was so socio-historically and culturally recognizable and significant and yet, nonetheless, could be construed as a failure, indeed a failure at language? This seemed to me to be the sort of question that should be central to applied linguistics, though at the time such questions were not seen as having anything to do with the field.

At another level this sharing-time data showed me a deep connection between oral language and literacy. Children at sharing time are being supported to talk, in some ways, the way they will later write in the case of things like essays. They are being supported by the teacher to say everything explicitly, to leave nothing to be inferred by their listeners on the basis of shared knowledge or context, and to organize everything around one clear and explicitly stated topic. Sharing time, as Michaels argued, was early training for a certain type of literacy, what Ron Scollon has called "essayist literacy" (Scollon & Scollon 1981; see Chapter 2 of this book).

It was clear that the type of talk teachers wanted at sharing time was not just any old talk. It was a special type of talk connected in integral ways with school and the sorts of reading and writing (literacy) schools most value. It became clear to me that it was important to study not just talk in general, but *different types of talk* connected to different purposes, goals, groups, practices, and institutions. It was important to study, as well, not just texts, but different types of writing connected to different purposes, goals, groups, practices, and institutions. All of a sudden literacy opened up as a very broad topic that crossed several different fields and encompassed individuals, society, institutions, and culture.

Leona had unwittingly been induced to bring the "wrong" type of talk to a school-based practice where it would get judged unfairly. In other contexts this type of talk would have been "right" and even "gifted." Indeed, it could have been "right" and "gifted" in an early creative storytelling session in school preparing children for creative literature. But sharing time was not that in these classrooms.

At a larger level, what Leona taught me is that we all need to know how to talk (and write) "right"—when and where to use certain ways with words—in order to count socially and culturally as "belonging." We all also need to know how others talk and write in contexts we too often misconstrue and, in the act, misrecognize what is "right" as "wrong."

Finally, we should not hide the social geography of talk and text, but make this geography overt. We must make it over not just for fairness and justice, but for new forms of collective intelligence that pool diversity in the name of human progress. Indeed, the study of literacy is about how talk and text are socially distributed as founding elements of our social lives and institutions.

Language

Linguists spend their time studying what language is and what it does. Different linguists study language in different ways. Some study the design features that the grammars of all the world's languages share. Some study the differences among languages. Some linguists focus on structure, others on meaning. Some linguists study language in the head, some study language in society.

At a general level, the study of language represents the dynamics between one and many. This dynamic characterizes a good many other things we academics study. What is English (or any other language)? In one sense, English is a set of common grammatical resources that the speakers of the language share. It is one.

For example, all speakers of English can change verbs into nouns: "Hornworms grow" → "Hornworm growth." Here the verb "grow," which names a process, is turned into the noun "growth" (which names a thing, in this case an abstract thing). English speakers can do this in many different ways: "walk

home" → "take a walk home," "refuse" → "refusal," "die →
death," and so forth).

The grammar of English is a set of common tools (ways
of using words) that all speakers of English can put to use to
make meaning. They are like the common color spectrum that
painters use or the common set of tools carpenters build with.
In that sense, English is one thing.

But different speakers use the grammar of English—the
tools for sentence construction that it offers—in different
ways in different contexts for different purposes. And, thus,
English is many. For example, consider the two sentences
below:

1.   Hornworms sure vary a lot in how well they grow.
2.   Hornworm growth exhibits a significant amount of
     variation.

Both these sentences use grammatical tools that all speakers of English can use (e.g., "grow" → "growth," "vary" →
"variation") with words they know in the language. However,
sentences (1) and (2) use English grammatical resources
(put them together) in different ways. They are different
styles of language used in different contexts and for different
purposes.

Sentence (2) is in an academic style of language and is used
in disciplines like biology. Sentence (1) is the sort of style some
people would use in informal talk in so-called "vernacular"
language. Of course, there are a great many other styles of language such as how lawyers speak when they are being lawyers,
how gang members speak when they are being gang members,
how people speak when they pray, and how (video) gamers
talk when they are being gamers.

So English is also many things, many different styles of speaking or writing. The different styles mean and portend different things. It is much like wearing clothes. If I put on a bathing suit, flip-flops, a tank-top, and a sun hat, the combination of my clothes says something like "beach time." If I wear a suit and tie and formal shoes, the combination says something like "professional" or "work time."

Not anything can go with anything. There are "rules" (conventions) about what can go with what. You don't usually wear a tie to the beach and, if you do, you are taken as trying to make a "statement" by flaunting the "rules." So, too, with language. Note that while sentence (1) can have the adverb "sure" in it (an "emotive" word showing excitement, for example that the speaker is impressed), this word cannot occur in sentence (2) without sounding odd:

3. Hornworm growth sure exhibits a significant amount of variation.

Sentence (3) is somewhat like wearing flip-flops as shoes with a formal suit. They just don't "go" with a suit and tie (if one wants to stick to the conventions of how "we" do things). At a deeper level, "sure" adds an element of informal language and emotion to a combination of words and grammatical units that is meant to betoken science as technical and rational.

Different dialects of English add, change, or subtract some tools in the grammatical tool-kit of English. A dialect is a style of language that reflects the common grammatical resources that a social or geographical sub-group of English speakers use (resources some of which not all English speakers have). So Leona's "my puppy be followin' me" uses a form "be followin'" that her dialect has and some other dialects of English do not have (including so-called "Standard English").

Leona's so-called "naked be" form ("be following") is what linguists call a habitual or durative aspect marker (Comrie 1976). "Aspect" means any grammatical device that indicates how events pattern in time. The "naked be" form is an aspect marker for happenings that are habitual or endure or repeat over time. Another aspect marker in English is "-ing," which means a happening is ongoing in time, as in "John is travelling to England" (so in Leona's dialect, "John be travelling to England" would mean he travels to England a lot or has been on the trip a long time).

Standard English has no such durative/habitual marker (though it once did), but a great many other languages in the world do. Leona's dialect has simply added a device (back) to the larger shared grammar of English. Such things are entirely common as all languages change through time.

Human groups change language all the time. They have ever done so. Physicists and mathematicians long ago combined words with mathematical symbols (in speech and writing). Today, thanks to modern social and digital media, young people are creating new styles of language by mixing and matching "natural language" with new symbols and new conventions. For example (see Gee & Hayes 2010 and Chapter 4 of this book):

Sunday, 02 December 2007
As u can see I gave my page a little makeover! I've had that oldd one for over a year! Needed a change! As 4 LH 1.3 I've got around thirty slides, working up to my usual 127! Patience is all it takes! I garentee it'll B out B4 Xmas though! ;)
    <3 A

It is crucial to see that, from a linguistic point of view, we must not compare one style of language to another in terms of better or worse—or say there are errors in a given style—until we have asked what work the style is meant to accomplish. A given style of language can only be judged in terms of the work it is meant to do. In the example from social media above (from a fifteen-year-old fan-fiction writer keeping in social contact with her large fan base) the "misspellings" and other features of the text are there for a specific form of social bonding and social identification. A misspelling in an essay means something entirely different and is most often a "mistake," since essays have different purposes, do different work.

Another Story

We have seen that a language or a dialect is something people share, something they have in common. Languages and dialects are also resources through which humans create diversity. This diversity allows them to accomplish different types of work and/or to identify themselves with different specific social or cultural groups.

The dance between commonality (unity) and diversity has long been vexed in society and in academic research. When commonality becomes an imposition that seeks to erase diversity or when diversity becomes a rallying cry for in-groupism, we get injustice, hatred, and even war.

When we study language, literacy, society, and culture—as we will in this book—we will deal a great deal with issues of commonality and diversity, inequality and justice, and belonging and isolation. In Education and the social sciences, a good many scholars greatly value diversity and are suspicious of calls for commonality and unity as imperialistic. Others in the academy and in society put a higher premium on commonality and fear the silos, isolation, and echo chambers that hiving off too many like-minded groups can create.

So let me end this introductory chapter by sharing with you a true story. The story is about commonality and diversity. Some years ago I was studying talk and interaction in a project where school teachers and university academics had come together to design an oral history curriculum for middle-school students in a post-industrial town in New England. The town had once been a flourishing blue-collar town, but had hit on hard times as industrial jobs had been out-sourced overseas (Gee 2014).

School teachers in this town were the products of 19th and 20th century white immigration. Their people had come from all over Europe, from places like Ireland, Poland, and Russia. The teachers were third-generation members of the town and they hoped their children would spend their lives there as well.

The university academics were from a private college in the town. None of them had been born in the town and many did not intend to end their careers there. They oriented to a national level of prestige and felt little shared cultural identity with the school teachers.

The school teachers felt that their immigrant ancestors had struggled to find a common identity as citizens of the town. They saw belonging to the town as an identity that transcended their immigrant differences. In fact, they saw their identity as citizens of the town as what gave them distinctiveness from the big city that defined the state they were in.

The town had a rich, long, and storied history. The teachers saw themselves and their families as having added to and continued this history through immigration, even though they were not part of the original English immigrants who had settled the town and America (actually, taken it from the native inhabitants).

Simultaneously with its loss of its industrial base, the town had experienced a massive new wave of "brown" immigrants. These new immigrants came from Mexico, South America, the Caribbean, and Asia. Both the loss of industry and this new immigration were caused by the new global economy that began in the late 1970s.

As the school teachers and the university academics talked in their meetings, one thing the academics were very concerned about was cultural diversity. They pressed to find out if the teachers—whose classrooms were filled with both white students and the new "brown" immigrants—honored diversity. At one point an academic asked a teacher whether she had "diversity" in her classroom. The teacher said, "No, they are all town kids," meaning they are all now "from our town," citizens of the town.

To the school teachers, all the kids in their classrooms were citizens of the town and it was the teachers' job to create a sense of common belonging and contribution to the town. The academics came to suspect the teachers were racists. The teachers thought that the academics obliterated the children's individual identities and needs under large group labels (e.g., African-American, Hispanic, Asian, and so forth).

In one meeting where the group was discussing classrooms and curriculum, the teachers used the word "common" or "commonality" dozens of time, but never used the words "diverse" or "diversity." The academics used the words "diverse" and "diversity" dozens of times, but never used the word "common" or "commonality."

For the teachers, common and commonwealth were good, while diversity was a macro-level phenomenon that academics studied but that could forestall seeing each child in a class as a town citizen in the making, able to carry on the history of the town as the teachers had themselves. For the academics, diversity was good and commonality was an imperialistic way to efface diversity. They talked for hours without ever rising to the meta-level to explicitly name their assumptions and compare and contrast them with mutual respect.

It is an irony that the town had schools integrated by race and class. The people in the town, the products of the earlier white immigration, wanted all citizens of the town together in school for fear of losing their town identity and history. In the big city that the town has defined itself against for such a long time—a much more prosperous and cosmopolitan place than the town—the schools were and are deeply segregated, as they are in so many other cities in the United States.

We will see in this book that diversity of many different sorts is essential for collective intelligence in school and society. But there is nothing for diversity to contribute to if we have no common projects as "citizens" of some sort—members of causes larger than ourselves and our "in-groups"—and as humans. Of course, we have to choose wisely.

2

LITERACY

Background: The 1980s

When I took my first job in a School of Education in 1982, that School, like most others, had a "Reading Program." The program trained people to teach reading, to engage in research on reading, and to carry out clinical practice on children with reading problems. Many of the reading courses had the word "remedial" in their titles. The going theory in those days was that most children learned to read well enough in school, but some had problems. These problems needed to be remediated, often in a reading clinic on campus in something akin to therapy. "Reading problems" were really the focus of the field.

Reading involves decoding (matching sounds and letters) and comprehension (understanding what one reads). However, reading researchers and clinicians have had a strong tendency to focus on decoding. There is a reason for this rooted in how reading works in the brain.

Work in reading research, psycholinguistics, and neuroscience has shown that the parts of the human brain that decode letters into sounds and sounds into letters is the only neural system germane just to reading itself (Shaywitz 2005). When we comprehend written language we use the very same parts of our brain that we use to comprehend oral language and, indeed, to understand things in the world. So decoding is the only mental capacity that is specific to reading (Stanovich 2000).

Decoding is a mental ability that is used only for languages that are written with alphabets (where letters represent sounds). Some languages are written with symbols that stand directly for meanings and not for sounds (e.g., Mandarin). For such languages, issues of decoding do not arise.

Comprehension is a general ability. One's abilities to comprehend oral language, written language, and events in the world all correlate with each other. Reading researchers tend to concentrate on specific comprehension strategies readers can use to become better readers, strategies such as monitoring one's understanding of a text, asking oneself questions about the text, and summarizing the text (Stanovich 2000). They do not delve more deeply into how human understanding works and what "feeds" or "starves" this far more basic human capacity in regard to oral language, written language, and the world. This is an issue we will take up in Chapter 3.

Reading and the Social World

In the 1980s reading was viewed primarily as a mental ability. However, reading scholars—like everyone else—knew that in the United States poor children and children from some (but not all) minority groups tended to learn to read later and less well than richer children and those children from other minority groups (Barton & Coley 2010) . This fact should have been seen as a great mystery. After all, why should poverty or a minority group membership affect how a child learns a skill like reading in school?

A story can indicate here how such social facts were a problem for the view that reading is a mental act. I was once, while giving a talk at a prestigious university, visiting with a leading faculty member there in reading. I pointed out that (though it was not a well-known fact) between 1970 and the early 1980s the white–black gap in reading test scores and on almost all other sorts of tests was fast declining. This progress stopped dead in the early 1980s (Barton & Coley 2010; Neisser 1998; Steele & Aronson 1998). It seemed important to know why the gap had been closing and why that progress stopped. Indeed, I claimed to the faculty member that this was an important reading research problem.

My colleague stopped me and said that this was not a reading problem, but a social one. I said, in return, that whatever had caused the progress made from 1970 to the early 1980s—since it was progress on reading tests and more progress than many other specific reading interventions had ever made—seemed to be a reading intervention and a successful one at that. My colleague disagreed. It had nothing to do with reading, he said, reading was a mental process, not a social one.

Even to this day, the reason the white–black gap was closing has not been much studied. This is quite surprising given how much energy educators of all types have spent on trying to close the white–black gap over the last few decades. The reason it was closing was probably due to the decrease in segregation caused, in part, by Lyndon Johnson's Great Society programs and the Civil Rights movement. Unfortunately, housing segregation today is as bad as it was in the 1960s.

But what could segregation have to do with reading? If reading is just a mental ability triggered by instruction and practice, then why should instruction lead to better results for some groups than for others? Other abilities, like learning to play music, play sports, play video games, speak foreign languages, cook, or count do not show any white–black differences, though they show individual differences.

Furthermore, about 80 percent of children learn to read regardless of the method of instruction used as long as it is one of the several different methods that work well (Snow, Burns, & Griffin 1998). It is understandable that children with specific disabilities may have trouble learning to read. But should children without disabilities have such trouble?

The view of reading current in the 1980s could not answer the question of why and how reading was so sensitive to divides in class and culture. Or, at least, the field, by and large, saw these issues as having nothing to do with reading directly. And, in one sense, they were right. If our view of reading does not stray too far from decoding and basic comprehension strategies, then it is hard to see how issues of class and culture can be very germane.

One other factor that caused social and cultural issues to be placed in the background in reading as a field was the fact that reading scholars focused almost primarily on reading (and writing) as things learned and used in school. How people read and wrote in their out-of-school lives did not draw much attention. What mattered is what happened in school.

This school focus would lead to a serious problem for claims made about the effects of literacy—claims about what good things literacy led to for people and countries. When scholars wanted to attribute effects to reading and writing—whether these were individual factors like growth in the ability to solve logical problems or nation-wide factors like economic growth—it was impossible to tell whether the claimed effects were due to literacy or schooling in general, since the two were rarely studied in isolation. It was not even clear whether the white–black, poor–rich gaps in reading had more to do with reading or with school as we know it.

The Effects of Literacy

It was ground-breaking work by Sylvia Scribner and Michael Cole in their book *The Psychology of Literacy* (1981) that first disentangled the effects of literacy (the ability to read and sometimes write) from the effects of schooling as we know it in the West. It had been assumed for centuries that literacy gives rise to higher-order cognitive abilities, such as more analytic and logical thought than is typical of oral cultures. However, this almost common-sense assumption was disputed by Scribner and Cole's work.

Scribner and Cole studied a people named the Vai, a small West African group that had developed their own system of writing. Among the Vai, literacy and schooling do not always go together. There are three sorts of literacy among the Vai, with some people having none, one, two, or all three types: (1) English literacy acquired in formal school settings of the Western sort; (2) an indigenous Vai script (a syllabic script, not an alphabetic one; that is, it is a script where written symbols represent syllables, not individual sounds) transmitted outside an institutional setting (i.e., among peers and family) and with no connection to Western-style schooling; and (3) a form of literacy in Arabic used for Islamic religious purposes (primarily to memorize and recite the Quran) acquired in Islamic religious schools.

Scribner and Cole found that neither syllabic Vai literacy nor Arabic literacy (the two settings that were outside of formal Western schooling) were associated with what have been considered higher-order intellectual skills as these are tested by our typical school-based tests. Neither of these types of literacy enhanced the use of taxonomic skills (abstract categorization skills), nor did either contribute to a shift toward syllogistic reasoning (logical reasoning). In contrast, literacy in English, the only form associated with formal schooling of the Western sort, was associated with some types of such abstract reasoning.

However, after English literates had been out of school a few years, they only did better than non-literates on verbal explanation tasks ("talking about" tasks). They did not any longer do better on actual problem solving, e.g., on categorization and abstract reasoning tasks. School skills, beyond talk, are transitory, unless they are repeatedly practiced in people's daily lives.

In the Scribner and Cole study, literacy in and of itself led to no grandiose cognitive abilities. And formal schooling ultimately led to quite specific abilities that are rather useless without institutions which reward "expository talk in contrived situations" (such as schools, courts, bureaucracies).

Scribner and Cole's work shows that many of the effects we often attribute to literacy are due to formal schooling of the Western sort. Consider a list (or set of pictures) like "wood, axe, hammer." Which of these "go together"? Vai who had not been to school, but who were literate in Vai script, would answer that the axe and wood go together because you use the axe to cut the wood. Schooled Vai would answer that the axe and hammer go together because they are tools. The former answered in terms of contexts of use, the latter in terms of abstract categories. (The actual test Scribner and Cole used is a bit different than this, but this makes the point more clearly.)

Scribner and Cole did find that school led people to be able to solve certain sorts of logical and abstract problems better. But this skill deteriorated soon after they left school, if they did not practice it in their work or daily lives. They could still talk a good game about such problems, but they were unable to actually solve them anymore. Such transitory effects of schooling have been found in the United States and other developed countries as well.

Scribner and Cole went on to argue that people learn by practice and what they learn by practice are specific skills embedded in the practice. Different types of literacy and different uses of literacy allow people to practice different skills and, thus, become good at different things.

Children working to memorize the Quran became good at memorizing. Children literate only in Vai were good at holding and manipulating words in their mind, something they practiced a good deal in reading a script that left no boundaries between words. Formally schooled Vai were good at abstract categorization and reasoning, and, in the end, they were good with certain types of talk about abstract matters. This is what they practiced in school. Finally, the Scribner and Cole work clearly shows that literacy has different effects based on the institutions or cultures that sponsor it (I will use the term "sponsor" a good bit. I am indebted to Brandt 2009 for this term in regard to literacy).

The Literacy Myth

Across history and across various cultures, literacy has seemed to many people something that makes people "higher" human beings (Graff 1979). Literate people are, it is widely believed, more intelligent, more modern, and more moral. Countries with high literacy rates are supposedly better developed, more modern, and better behaved.

It has been argued that literacy is what freed some of humanity from a "primitive" state, from an earlier stage of human development in which there was no writing. If language is what makes us all human, literacy was believed to be what makes some of us "civilized" (Goody 1977, 1986; Goody & Watt 1963; Graff 1979, 1981a, b; 1987a, b; Olson 1977; Ong 1982; Pattison 1982; Scribner & Cole 1981). Furthermore, just as some people today have claimed that digital media have changed the human mind, so, too, literacy was held to create a great divide between the "literate mind" and the "illiterate mind."

There has been a very long list of claims for the powers of literacy: Literacy leads to logical, analytical, critical, and rational thinking; general and abstract uses of language; skeptical and questioning attitudes; a distinction between myth and history; a recognition of the importance of time and space; complex and modern governments (with separation of church and state); political democracy and greater social equity; a lower crime rate; better citizens; economic development, wealth and productivity; political stability; urbanization; and a lower birth rate.

However, in the 1980s some scholars began to dispute this omnipotent view of literacy. They referred to it as "the literacy myth" (Graff 1979, 1987a, b). They argued that there is, in fact, little historical evidence for these claims about literacy. This is because the role of literacy is always more complex and contradictory and more deeply intertwined with other factors than the literacy myth allows.

This point is well made by a consideration of the first country in the West to achieve near-universal literacy: Sweden.

Sweden accomplished this feat before the 18th century (Graff 1987b). Sweden was also unprecedented in that women had equality with men in literacy, an equality that still does not exist in most of the world today.

By the tenets of the literacy myth, Sweden should have been an international example of modernization, social equality, economic development, and cognitive growth. But it was no such thing.

Sweden's remarkable achievement took place in a land of widespread poverty and, for the most part, without the help of formal schooling. Sweden's achievement of universal (reading) literacy did not follow from, nor stimulate any, significant economic development. Sweden achieved its impressive level of reading without writing. Writing did not become a part of popular literacy anywhere until the mid-nineteenth century and is still much less common across the world than is reading.

So how did Sweden manage the feat of universal literacy? The Swedish literacy campaign, one of the most successful in the Western world, was stimulated by the Reformation and Lutheran Protestantism. Teaching was done on a household basis led by mothers (hence the emphasis on the literacy of women), supervised and reinforced by the parish church and clergy, with regular compulsory examinations (Johansson 1977; Graff 1987b: 149).

The goal of literacy in Sweden was the promotion of Christian faith and life, as well as the promotion of character and citizenship training in a religiously dominated state. Religious, social, and political ideologies were transmitted to nearly everyone through literacy learning.

The Church Law of 1686 stated that children, farmhands, and maid-servants should "learn to read and see with their own eyes what God bids and commands in His Holy Word"

(Graff 1987b: 150). Note the phrase "with their own eyes": literally they see it with their own eyes, figuratively they see it through the eyes of the state church which dictates how it is to be taught and seen.

A common dilemma with literacy arises here: People are given a text for themselves, but then something must ensure they see it "right," not in reality through their own eyes, but rather from the perspective of an authoritative institution that delimits correct interpretations. Clearly, in these cases, the individual reader does not need any very deep comprehension skills and surely doesn't need to be able to write.

This problem—that people might not see the text in the "right" way—was a problem in both Protestant and Catholic countries, but the two hit on different solutions. Catholic-dominated countries were much more reluctant to put the Bible and other sacred texts into the hands of the people, for fear they would not interpret them correctly (for example, they might use them as the basis for political or religious dissent). Catholic countries preferred to leave interpretation to the oral instruction of church authorities. When the Catholic Church did allow sacred texts into the hands of the people, it attempted to fix their meanings by orthodox exposition (e.g., sermons) and standardized religious illustrations (Graff 1987b: 147).

As a result of these attitudes, Catholic countries tended to be culturally and economically behind areas of intense Protestant piety (such as Sweden, lowland Scotland, New England, Huguenot French centers, and places within Germany and Switzerland). So there was something happening with literacy in the hands of the people, even if it was only literacy to build religious faith and living. But the sort of literacy in 18th and 19th century Sweden and a Catholic country with quantitatively more restricted literacy were both based on dominant modes of interpretation sponsored by powerful religious and civil institutions. And neither Protestant nor Catholic countries were modern, humane, or rational in any recognizable sense.

Of course, literacy cannot have any effects if it is not actually in the hands of people, if they cannot read and write, as they could not in the Catholic countries. The great literacy scholar and activist Paulo Freire (1970) has argued that literacy can be emancipatory. Literacy, he claimed, has the capacity to give rise to dissent and critical awareness. However, this capacity was not much exercised in either 18th and 19th century Catholic France and Protestant Sweden. So, if literacy has the capacity for dissent and critical awareness, something beyond literacy itself must trigger this capacity or serve as a catalyst for it. We will discuss Freire later below.

Eric Havelock and Greece

We have come to the point where we clearly face the unity/ diversity (one/many) issue for literacy. Is literacy one thing with predictable effects (or at least affordances) or is it many different things in different contexts and cultures?

Eric Havelock (1976) and Walter Ong (1982) have been the two most influential scholars who have made strong claims for the general (and sweeping) effects of literacy. They both view literacy as a powerful force for social transformation.

The case of Sweden has already indicated the sorts of complexity that can arise when we make general claims for literacy. But the work of Havelock and Ong shows us some deep possibilities and affordances of literacy, as, too, will Freire's work below. Before we consider how to resolve the one/many question for literacy, we need to consider this work.

Homeric Greek culture was an oral (non-literate) culture. Havelock's (1976) characterization of that culture has been used both as a characterization of oral cultures generally and as a cornerstone in the argument that it is literacy that makes for a "great divide" between human cultures and their ways of thinking (oral versus literate).

The Greek oral epic—such as the *Iliad* and the *Odyssey* in their original forms as oral stories—was a storehouse of social directives. Havelock calls it an "encyclopedia of conduct" in the form of poetic and memorized speech. The oral epic was the way Greek culture passed down its values and knowledge in the absence of writing.

Havelock argues that the epic took the form it did due to the demands of human memory without writing (writing is a sort of external memory storage device). The epic was recited with a heavy metrical rhythm. It was constructed out of a large set of pre-given, memorized formulae (short phrases that would fit the meter), as well as a large set of pre-given motifs (stereotypical characters, actions, and events) and wider themes, each of which recurred throughout the epic (Finnegan 1977, 1988; Foley 1988; Lord 1960; Parry 1971). The epic was dramatic poetry.

There was, however, still scope for creativity. These building blocks were arranged and ordered somewhat differently on any occasion of recitation. Recitation was always sensitive to the reactions of the audience.

An epic poet (one of the many "Homers" who earned their living singing tales) might be reciting the epic at dinner for a group of aristocrats and could add material relevant to their ancestors or accomplishments. The singer of tales could shorten or lengthen the epic in light of the audience's enthusiasm or lack of it. The epic was often recited accompanied by music played on a one-stringed instrument. The epic poet was a performer.

Oral poetry constituted didactic entertainment. If it ceased to entertain, it ceased to be effectively didactic. It was rhythm that underlay the pleasure people took in the epic: the rhythm of recurrent meter, formulae, motifs, and themes. The epic was a type of music in words.

Furthermore, Havelock argues that the knowledge in an oral culture was compelled to heed the psychological requirements of human memory. Human memory works best for stories and stories are built from actions and actors, not abstractions and principles. Havelock argues that this kind of discourse represents "the limits within which the mind of the members of that culture can express itself, the degree of sophistication to which they can attain" (Havelock 1976: 182).

Havelock argues that the teller of tales and his audience were under a "spell." The epic poet was under the spell of the epic rhythm created by meter and recurrent themes. Listeners entered the spell, too, as they identified with the rhythm and the telling of the tale. The epic was an acting out of and an identification with the values and beliefs of the society. Innovation in values and ideas was difficult. The cost of giving up what one has memorized and memorizing anew was just too great.

Plato was one of the first great writers of Greek civilization. He sought to relocate power away from the epic poets and their tales to philosopher kings. In the earlier oral culture, it was the Homeric poet who was the keeper of history and knowledge. Plato wanted to replace the poet as the keeper of knowledge with written language and philosophy (prose). To do so he had to break the power of the epic poet ("Homer"), because in the poet's care resided the moral and intellectual heritage of the society. Thus, it is no surprise that in Plato's "perfect" society, described in *The Republic*, he excludes poets ("Homer").

What woke the Greeks from the spell cast by the epic poets? Havelock's answer: alphabetic-script literacy, a profoundly changed technology of communication. Written language allows people to store and refresh memory. People could dispense with the emotional identification (the "spell") by which the oral epic story ensured recall. This could release cognitive energy for a review and rearrangement of what had now been written down.

An oral epic is heard fleetingly through time. It is hard to recall what was said earlier and hard to compare and contrast different parts of the epic as they flow through time, often for hours. However, what has been written down can be seen as an object (a "text") and not just heard and felt. The reader can take a second look. The reader of prose can compare and contrast distant parts of the text and find contradictions and inconsistencies, undeterred by the emotional sway of rhythm and the dramatic action.

In Plato's dialogues, Socrates asks the epic poets what their poems mean. This request demands that the poets say again what the poems say, but in prose this time, not poetry. The poets became his victims. What had sounded so compelling in poetry did not seem so in prose.

The Greek cultural tradition in moral, social, and historical matters was in the keeping of the poets and their poetry. They owned the tribal encyclopedia. To ask what it was saying amounted to a demand that it be said differently, non-poetically, non-rhythmically, and non-imagistically. In the act, the spell was broken. What Plato was helping to create was an abstract language of prose (and a sort of descriptive science) to replace the concrete poetic language of oral memory (Havelock 1976: 209).

The case of Sweden and many other historical cases show that the situation in Greece was not as general as Havelock argues. It was special in certain ways to Greece in that historical period. Nonetheless, we can ask if Havelock has uncovered certain affordances that literacy can have, in the right set of circumstances, to undo the work of what Plato called "speech-writers." For Plato, "speech-writers" were rhetoricians, politicians, and court poets who used the power of language to persuade and support power even in the absence of evidence and truth. Speech-writers are with us to this day.

Walter Ong

Walter Ong's seminal and entertaining book *Orality and Literacy* (1982) is also a sweeping statement about orality and literacy as a great divide in human thought and history. Work on oral and literate cultures, Ong argues, has made us revise our understanding of human identity. Writing—commitment of the word to space—enlarges the potentiality of language "almost beyond measure" and "restructures thought":

> Oral cultures indeed produce powerful and beautiful verbal performances of high artistic and human worth, which are no longer even possible once writing has taken possession of the psyche. Nevertheless, without writing, human consciousness cannot achieve its fuller potentials, cannot produce other beautiful and powerful creations. In this sense, orality needs to produce and is destined to produce writing.
>
> Literacy, as will be seen, is absolutely necessary for the development not only of science but also history, philosophy, explicative

understanding of literature and of any art, and indeed for the explanation of language (including oral speech) itself. There is hardly an oral culture or a predominantly oral culture left in the world today that is not somehow aware of the vast complex of powers forever inaccessible without literacy. This awareness is agony for persons rooted in primary orality, who want literacy passionately but who also know very well that moving into the exciting world of literacy means leaving behind much that is exciting and deeply loved in the earlier oral world. We have to die to continue living.

(pp. 14–15)

Ong's book offers a strong characterization of thought and expression in oral cultures. But Ong also makes a crucial move when he claims that "to varying degrees many cultures and subcultures, even in a high-technology ambiance, preserve much of the mind-set of primary orality" (p. 11). And, indeed, many of the features of oral cultures Ong cites have been found to be characteristic of, for instance, some of the oral-culture-like language practices in parts of African-American culture. Some African-American people, though they are literate, still have ties to a former rich oral culture, both from the days of slavery in the U.S. and from African cultures (Baugh 1983, 1999; Labov 1972; Mufwene, Rickford, Bailey, & Baugh 1998; Rickford & Rickford 2000; Smitherman 1977; Stucky 1987).

Ong claims that many modern cultures which have known writing for centuries have not fully interiorized it. He uses as examples Arabic culture and certain other Mediterranean cultures (e.g., ironically, after Havelock's work, including modern Greek culture).

Ong also points out that oral habits of thought and expression, including massive use of formulaic elements of a type similar to those in Homer, still marked prose style of almost every sort in Tudor England, some two thousand years after Plato's campaign in writing against oral poets. Thus, the range of application of Ong's contrast between literacy and orality is greatly expanded by his inclusion of groups with what he refers to as "residual orality" on the oral side of the dichotomy.

The set of features that Ong offers as characteristic of thought and expression in a primary oral culture are these:

1. Expanding on Havelock, the first feature Ong offers is "formulaic thought and expression," defined as "more or less exactly repeated set phrases or set expressions (such as proverbs)" (p. 26).
2. Thought and expression in an oral culture are additive (strung together by additive relations like "and") rather than subordinative (complex forms of grammatical embedding).
3. They are aggregative (elements of thought or expression come in clusters, e.g., not "the princess" but "the beautiful princess") rather than analytic.
4. They are redundant or "copious" with much repetition and repetition with variation.
5. They are conservative or traditionalist, inhibiting experimentation.
6. They are close to the human life world in the sense that they are agonistically toned; empathetic and participatory rather than objectively distanced; situational rather than abstract.

Though Ong restricts these features to primary rather than residually oral cultures, it is striking how similar some of these features are to characterizations linguists have offered of the differences between speech and writing, educators have offered of the differences between so-called "bad" and "good" writers, and sociolinguists have offered of differences between forms of prosaic versus poetic storytelling (Bauman & Sherzer 1974; Michaels 1981).

Thus we get to one of the main implications of the Havelock–Ong line of work. In modern technological societies like the U.S. something akin to the oral–literate distinction may still apply between groups with "residual orality" or "restricted literacy." Residual orality means these groups still have a deep commitment to face-to-face forms of rhythmic storytelling and other poetic forms of oral expression. Restricted literacy means, in practice, that some groups have low allegiance to the types of literacy practices schools value, though they may have their own literacy practices. The terms are unfortunate. I would prefer "retained orality" and "lowered allegiance to school-based literacy."

Ong anticipated the way in which today digital media (virtually non-existent at the time he wrote) have created what Ong referred to as "secondary orality." On social media we see forms of writing that include properties we associate with speech. People having real-time chats, for instance, are writing in order to "talk" (converse). There are, of course, a wide variety of "talk-like" interactions made possible by social media. Is it possible that such practices will lead to new forms of "orality" (for example, new forms of person-to-person real-time conversation) and perhaps, too, less allegiance, in some cases, to school-based literacy and forms like the essay?

While Ong celebrates literacy, he is aware that any new technology reorders old ones. In the process, some good things are always lost or attenuated. Ong is well aware of the power of the poetic mind. And, too, modern memories are weak indeed compared to those of our ancestors in oral cultures.

At the same time, both Ong and Havelock, in my view, see literacy as too monolithic. Neither considers the way in which literacy (reading and writing) inside specific social, cultural, and institutional practices may have quite different effects, good or bad. They both indicate powerful potentials (or affordances) which literacy has—for good and bad—but not the nuances of context and the necessary sponsors or catalysts for literacy to have certain sorts of effects (as religion did in Sweden).

Brian Street

In line with the work of Scribner and Cole, the anthropologist Brian Street (1984) launched a trenchant critique against sweeping claims for literacy. He says that claims that literacy (or schooling, for that matter) has cognitive effects apart from the context in which it exists and the uses to which it is put in a given culture represent a (mistaken) "autonomous model" of literacy.

Claims for literacy, for example for the effects of essay-text literacy ("school literacy" as we know it), are, Street argues, "ideological" (belief-based and value-laden). They are part of a set of concepts, conventions, and practices that privilege one social formation (e.g., various forms of religion, schooling, or the state) as if it were natural, universal, or, at the least, the end point of a normal developmental progression (achieved only by some cultures, thanks either to their intelligence or their technology).

Street proposes, in opposition to the "autonomous model" of literacy, an "ideological model." The ideological model attempts to understand literacy in terms of concrete social practices and to theorize it in terms of the ideologies (beliefs

and value systems) in which different literacies are embedded. For Street, literacy—of whatever type—only has consequences as it acts together with a large number of other social
and cultural factors, including political and economic conditions, social structure, and local ideologies.

Any technology, including writing, is a cultural form. It is a
social product whose shape and influence depend upon prior
political and ideological factors. Despite Havelock's brilliant
characterization of the transition from orality to literacy in
ancient Greece, it now appears that the Greek situation has
rarely if ever been replicated. The particular social, political,
economic and ideological circumstances in which literacy
(of a particular sort) was embedded in Greece explain what
happened there. Abstracting literacy from its social setting
in order to make claims for literacy as an autonomous force
in shaping the mind or a culture simply leads to a dead end,
Street argues.

There is, however, a last refuge for someone who wants to
see literacy as an autonomous force. One could claim that
essay-text literacy and the uses of language connected with it
lead, if not to general cognitive consequences, to social mobil-
ity and success in the society. While this argument may be
true, there is precious little evidence that literacy in history or
across cultures has always had this effect either.

Street discusses, in this regard, Harvey Graff's (1979) study
of the role of literacy in 19th century Canada. While some
individuals did gain through the acquisition of literacy, Graff
demonstrates that this was not a statistically significant effect.
Deprived classes and ethnic groups as a whole were, if anything, further oppressed through literacy. Greater literacy did
not correlate with increased equality and democracy, nor with

better conditions for the working class, but in fact with continuing social stratification.

Graff argues that the teaching of literacy in fact involved a contradiction: illiterates were considered dangerous to the social order, thus they must be made literate. Yet the potentialities of reading and writing for an under-class could well be radical and inflammatory. So the framework for the teaching of literacy had to be severely controlled in terms of how literacy was taught (the pedagogy) and the values that were taught with it. Indeed, this debate—how to make people literate without making them too critical of current power structures—goes on to this day.

While the workers were led to believe that acquiring literacy was to their benefit, Graff produces statistics that show that in reality this literacy was not advantageous to the poorer groups in terms of either income or power. The extent to which literacy was an advantage or not in relation to job opportunities depended on ethnicity. It was not because you were "illiterate" that you finished up in the worst jobs, but because of your background (e.g., being black or Irish Catholic rendered literacy much less efficacious than it was for English Protestants).

The story Graff tells can be repeated for many other societies, including Britain and the United States (Donald 1983; Levine 1986). In all these societies, literacy served as a socializing tool for the poor, was seen as a possible threat if misused by the poor (for an analysis of their oppression and to make demands for power), and served as a technology for the continued selection of members of one class for the best positions in the society.

But does this mean that literacy cannot be emancipatory? For this issue we must turn to Paulo Freire.

Freire and Emancipatory Literacy

No figure is more associated with the emancipatory capacities of literacy than is Paulo Freire (1970, 1973, 1985; Freire & Macedo 1987). Up to this point, we have concentrated on the authoritarian side of literacy, the desire and need for the powerful to enforce interpretations. But Freire argues there is another side to literacy, the liberating side, an emancipatory literacy for religious, political, and cultural resistance to domination. The historian Harvey Graff acknowledges this side to literacy:

> Literacy was one of the core elements of England's centuries-old radical tradition. In the context of a complex interweaving of political, cultural, social, and economic changes, an essentially new element in literacy's history was formed: the association of literacy with radical political activities, as well as with "useful knowledge," one of the many factors in the making of an English working class . . . Reading and striving for education helped the working class to form a political picture of the organization of their society and their experience in it.
>
> (Graff 1987b: 324)

Freire believed that literacy only empowers people when it renders them active questioners of the social reality around them:

> Reading the world always precedes reading the word, and reading the word implies continually reading the world . . . In a way, however, we can go further and say that reading the word is not preceded merely by reading the world, but by a certain form of writing it or rewriting it, that is, of transforming it by means of conscious, practical work. For me, this dynamic movement is central to the literacy process.
>
> (Freire & Macedo 1987: 35)

In a chapter entitled "The People Speak Their Word: Literacy in Action" in his book with Donaldo Macedo, Freire discusses and cites material from learner workbooks he helped design for a national literacy campaign in the republic of São Tomé and Príncipe. This was a nation that had recently freed itself from "the colonial yoke to which it was subjected for centuries" (p. 65).

The second Notebook begins by "provoking a debate" (p. 76) and goes on to say to the learner: "To study is not easy, because to study is to create and re-create and not to repeat what others say" (p. 77). The Notebook tells the learner that education is meant to develop "a critical spirit and creativity, not passivity" (p. 91). Freire says that in these materials "one does not particularly deal with delivering or transferring to the people more rigorous explanations of the facts, as though these facts were finalized, rigid, and ready to be digested. One is concerned with stimulating and challenging them" (p. 78).

All this sounds liberating. But there's another note here as well. Freire comes up square against the old problem: what is to ensure that when people read (either a text or the world) they will do so "correctly"? Thus, the second Notebook also reads:

> When we learn to read and write, it is also important to learn to think correctly. To think correctly we should think about our practice in work. We should think about our daily lives.
>
> (p. 76)

> Our principal objective in writing the texts of this Notebook is to challenge you, comrades, to think correctly.
>
> (p. 87)

> Now try to do an exercise, attempting to think correctly. Write on
> a piece of paper how you see this problem: "Can the education of
> children and adults, after the Independence of our country, be equal
> to the education that we had before Independence?"
>
> (p. 88)

> Let's think about some qualities that characterize the new man and
> the new woman. One of these qualities is agreement with the Peo-
> ple's cause and the defense of the People's interests . . . The correct
> sense of political militancy, in which we are learning to overcome
> individualism and egoism, is also a sign of the new man and the
> new woman.
>
> To study (a revolutionary duty), to think correctly . . . all these are
> characteristics of the new man and the new woman.
>
> (p. 92)

It is, perhaps, striking that a pedagogy that Freire says is "more a pedagogy of question than a pedagogy of answer," a pedagogy that is radical because it is "less certain of certainties" (p. 54), in fact knows what it is to think correctly. Learners are told not to repeat what others say, but then the problem becomes that in "re-saying" what they read for themselves, they may say it wrong, i.e., conflict with Freire's or the state's political perspective. Thus, the literacy materials must ensure that they think correctly, that is, "re-say" or interpret text and world "correctly."

Freire was well aware that no literacy is politically neutral, including the institutionally based literacy of church, state, business, and school that has undergirded the hegemonic process in Western society, and continues to do so. Literacy always comes with a perspective on interpretation that is ultimately political. One can hide that perspective the better to claim it is not there, or one can put it out in the open. Plato, Sweden, Freire: all have a strong perspective on literacy. One thing that makes both Plato and Freire great is that neither attempts to hide his political perspective or to pretend that politics can be separated from literacy.

Whether we like Freire's or Plato's politics or not, the fact remains that there is a deep problem with the interpretation of texts: If no interpretation is better than any other, then all are equally good, anything goes, and no interpretation matters. If there have to be some interpretations that are more correct than others—and how could there not be, given that language is a set of shared conventions and authors have intentions?—then something has to determine or help guide what is a better interpretation and what a worse one.

We cannot escape the reality that any form of reading, whether reading texts or the world, is social. We share inter-pretations with others who have worked to form them, sup-port them, and nourish them. Therefore, while there may never be only one right way to interpret, there are not indefi-nitely many. We can vary on and even transform interpretative practices that have come before us, but we cannot, as an indi-vidual, wholly create new meanings. Some others must accept and follow our creation or it is still-born. There is no way out of debating interpretations in terms of norms and values that belong to social and cultural groups, large and small, and to worldviews, and to political projects.

In the end, we might say that, contrary to the literacy myth, nothing follows from literacy or schooling. Much follows, however, from what comes with literacy and schooling, what literacy and schooling come wrapped up in, namely the atti-tudes, values, norms, and beliefs (at once social, cultural, and political) that always accompany literacy and schooling. These consequences may be work habits that facilitate industrialization, abilities in "expository talk in contrived situations," a religiously or politically quiescent population, radical opposition to colonial oppressors, and any number of other things.

A text, whether written on paper, or on the soul (Plato), or on the world (Freire), is a loaded weapon. The person, the educator, who hands over the gun (the text), hands over the bullets (the interpretive perspective), and must own up to the consequences. There is no way out of having an opinion, an ideology, and a strong one, as did Plato, as did Freire. Literacy education is not for the timid.

When I originally wrote about Paulo Freire (1921–1997) in these terms, he was still alive. He was a man I had the great privilege to know personally. Freire was a towering figure, as an intellectual and as a person. Some people have taken the sorts of ideas presented here about Freire as a criticism of his work. I have not intended them as such: they are meant to be a reflection on the strength of mind both Plato and Freire had to confront the nature of literacy and the need to acknowledge openly and honestly the role of values, ideology, and worldviews. Literacy involves real dilemmas and both Plato and Freire confronted them head on.

Freire, in his classic book *The Pedagogy of the Oppressed* (1970), argued for a number of points that are as important today as when he first made them. Indeed, they are integral to the arguments about language and literacy I make in this book. And I will show in Chapter 3 that there is ample empirical evidence for these claims:

1. A "banking model" of learning does not work. By a "banking model," Freire meant a model where learning is seen as a "teacher" transmitting information to a "student."

Learning involves an active engagement with the world, with words, and with other people. It is not just about information. It is about actions, dialogue, producing knowledge, and changing ourselves and the world, as well.

2. "Reading the world" and "reading the word" are deeply similar—at some level, equivalent—processes. One cannot learn to "read the word" (make sense of a text) in some domain unless one has learned to "read the world" (make sense of the world that text is about) in that domain. How one "reads the word" and how one "reads the world" are heavily dependent on each other. They are inextricably interdependent.

3. Dialogue (that is, both face-to-face conversational interaction and conversation-like interaction at a distance through reflection on what one has heard or read) in which diverse viewpoints and perspectives are juxtaposed is, at several levels, essential for learning to "read the world" and to "read the word." Literacy cannot, then, be defined primarily in terms of either "private" individuals (and their mental states) or single isolated texts. Multiple and diverse perspectives juxtaposed in talk or in reflection are essential to literacy for Freire. This does not mean, however, that we can avoid living with and acting on our own values and perspectives, hopefully ones formed through study and reflection.

4. "Politics" (in the sense of assumptions, attitudes, values, and perspectives about the distribution of "social goods" in society, where, by "social goods," I mean anything that is considered good, appropriate, or right to have, do, or be in the society) does not stand outside of and is not peripheral to literacy. Rather, politics, in the sense just given, and literacy are integrally and inextricably interwoven.

This is so because "reading the world" always involves an interpretation of the "way things are" in terms of what is appropriate, normal, natural, or right in regard to the distribution of social goods. Since "reading the world" and "reading the word" are inextricably interwoven, so, too, then, are politics and literacy.

Rest in peace, dear Paulo Freire. May the next Freire be among the readers of this book.

Ron Scollon

So, we come to this: literacy has no effects—indeed, no meaning—apart from particular social, institutional, political, and cultural contexts in which it is used. And it has different effects in different contexts and cultures. In fact, learning a new type of literacy—new literacy practices—can, like learning a new language, become a matter of a change of identity and culture. One important book that helped initiate this perspective was Ronald and Suzanne Scollon's *Narrative, Literacy, and Face in Interethnic Communication* (1981). The Scollons argue that what is at issue in the use of language is different ways of knowing and different ways of making sense of the world of human experience.

The Scollons believe that discourse patterns (ways of using language to communicate, whether in speech or writing) in different cultures reflect particular reality sets or worldviews adopted by these cultures. Discourse patterns are among the strongest expressions of personal and cultural identity.

The Scollons argue that changes in a person's discourse patterns—for example, in acquiring a new form of literacy—often involve a change in a person's identity. They provide a detailed study of the discourse practices and worldview of Athabaskans in Alaska and northern Canada. They contrast these with the discourse patterns and worldview in much of Anglo-Canadian and Anglo-American society (see also Wieder & Pratt 1990a, b).

Literacy as it is practiced in European-based education, what the Scollons call "essay-text" literacy, is connected to a reality set or worldview the Scollons call "modern consciousness." This reality set is consonant with particular discourse patterns, ones quite different from the discourse patterns used by the Athabaskans. As a result, the acquisition of this sort of literacy is not simply a matter of learning a new meaning-making technology for Athabaskans. It also involves complicity with values, social practices, and ways of knowing that conflict with those of the Athabaskans.

Athabaskans differ at various points from mainstream Canadian and American English speakers in how they engage in discourse. Here are a few examples:

1. Athabaskans have a high degree of respect for the individuality of others and they carefully guard their own individuality. Thus, they prefer to avoid conversation except when the point of view of all participants is well known. On the other hand, English speakers feel that the main way to get to know the point of view of people is through conversation with them.

2. For Athabaskans, people in subordinate positions do not display; rather, they observe the person in the superordinate position. For instance, adults as either parents or teachers are supposed to display abilities and qualities for the child to learn. However, in mainstream American society, children are supposed to show off their abilities for teachers and other adults.

3. The English idea of "putting your best foot forward" conflicts directly with an Athabaskan taboo. It is normal in situations of unequal status relations, for an English speaker, to display oneself in the best light possible. One will speak highly of the future, as well. It is normal to present a career or life trajectory of success and planning. This English system is very different from the Athabaskan system in which it is considered inappropriate and bad luck to anticipate good luck, to display oneself in a good light, to predict the future, or to speak badly of another's luck.

The Scollons list many other differences. These include differences in systems of pausing that ensure that English speakers select most of the topics and do most of the talking in interethnic encounters. The net result of these communication problems is that each group ethnically stereotypes the other. English speakers come to believe that Athabaskans are unsure, aimless, incompetent, and withdrawn. Athabaskans come to believe that English speakers are boastful, sure they can predict the future, careless with luck, and far too talkative.

The Scollons characterize the different discourse practices of Athabaskans and English speakers in terms of two different worldviews or "forms of consciousness": bush consciousness (connected with survival values in the bush) and modern consciousness. These forms of consciousness are "reality sets" in the sense that they are cognitive orientations toward the everyday world including learning in that world.

Anglo-Canadian and American mainstream culture has adopted a model of literacy (based on the values of essayist prose style) that is highly compatible with modern consciousness. In essayist prose, the important relationships to be signaled are those between sentence and sentence, not those between speakers, nor those between sentence and speaker. For a reader this requires a constant monitoring of grammatical and lexical information. With the heightened emphasis on truth value rather than social or rhetorical conditions comes the necessity to be explicit about logical implications.

A further significant aspect of essayist prose style is the fictionalization of both the audience and the author. The "reader" of an essayist text is not an ordinary human being, but an idealization, a rational mind formed by the rational body of knowledge of which the essay is a part. By the same token the author is a fiction, since the process of writing and editing essayist texts leads to an effacement of individual and idiosyncratic identity.

Essay-text literacy is about one rational mind communicating with another, not about idiosyncratic individuals communicating. The Scollons show the relation of these essayist values to modern consciousness by demonstrating that they are variants of the defining properties of modern consciousness as given by Berger, Berger, and Kellner (1973).

For the Athabaskan, writing in this essayist mode can constitute a *crisis in ethnic identity*. To produce an essay would require the Athabaskan to produce a major display, which would be appropriate only if the Athabaskan was in a position of dominance in relation to the audience. But the audience and the author are fictionalized in essayist prose and the text becomes decontextualized. This means that a contextualized, social relationship of dominance is obscured. Where the relationship of the communicants is unknown, the Athabaskan prefers silence.

The paradox of prose for the Athabaskan, then, is that if it is communication between known author and audience it is contextualized and compatible with Athabaskan values, but not good essayist prose. To the extent that it becomes decontextu-alized and thus good essayist prose, it becomes uncharacteristic of Athabaskans to seek to communicate. The Athabaskan set of discourse patterns are to a large extent mutually exclusive of the discourse patterns of essayist prose.

The Scollons go on to detail a number of narrative and non-narrative uses of language in Athabaskan culture, show-ing how each of these is in turn shaped by the Athabaskan "reality set," especially their respect for the individual and care about not overly intervening in others' affairs (including in their knowledge and beliefs). For example, riddles are an important genre in Athabaskan culture. Riddles are seen as schooling in guessing meanings, in reading between the lines, in anticipating outcomes and in indirectness. In short, riddles provide a schooling in non-intervention.

And in the best telling of an Athabaskan narrative, "little more than the themes are suggested and the audience is able to inter-pret those themes as highly contextualized in his own experi-ences" (Scollon & Scollon 1981: 127). This is, of course, just the reverse of the decontextualization valued by essayist prose.

The Scollons were not arguing, of course, that Athabaskans should not gain new forms of literacy and culture. Everyone in the modern world needs to do this. They were arguing that the processes of acquiring new forms of literacy—and new ways with words more generally—are also processes of acquir-ing new identities. When we teach or learn literacy we need to be cognizant of and sensitive to old identities as they interact with new ones.

The Scollons were also arguing that in multicultural set-tings in school and society we need to be aware that differ-ent cultures' favored ways of communicating are tied up with their values and identities. We need all of us to become meta-aware about—applied linguists of—cultural differences and not assume the other person is doing a "wrong" version of what we do, but a "right" version of what they do. Of course, in the act, we can become more aware of ourselves, of our own identities, something Socrates recommended.

Ron Scollon, too, is now gone (1939–2009). He was one of the best linguists and discourse analysts in the world. In so many respects he led the way—often not acknowledged nearly enough, partly because of his aversion to self-advertisement—for so many of the rest of us.

Ron told me once that he had not been interested in literacy or schooling until he took a job in Alaska (he later worked in Hong Kong and at Georgetown University). What struck him in Alaska was how aspects of literacy and school that so many of us take for granted were as alien to the Athabaskans as if an alien spaceship had landed in their midst.

Rest in peace, dear Ron Scollon. May the next Ron Scollon be among the readers of this book.

The New Literacy Studies (NLS)

In this chapter we have seen two dilemmas about literacy. First, in the 1980s—and often today as well—reading and writing were treated as mental abilities and studied in terms of what went on in minds/brains. Yet these mental abilities are exquisitely sensitive to social and cultural contexts and seem always inextricably linked to them.

Second, we have seen that literacy has a myriad of important social effects that have transformed society and history and even human identity. But these effects are different in the contexts of different practices in which literacy is used or to which literacy is relevant. Further, literacy has different effects depending on what sorts of institutions and interests sponsor it for specific goals and effects at local, national, or global levels.

Some of the work we have looked at in this chapter—work by Scriber and Cole, Graff, Street, and the Scollons—was part of a body of research that came to be called "the New Literacy Studies." In the 1980s a number of scholars from different disciplines began to critique the traditional view of literacy as "the ability to read and write" (a largely individual and mental phenomenon) and argue for a practice-based approach to literacy. These scholars studied reading and writing in their different social, cultural, institutional, and historical contexts (Barton 1994; Barton & Hamilton 1998; Cook-Gumperz 1986; Gee 1985, 1989; Graff 1979, 1987a, b; Gumperz 1982a, b; Heath 1982, 1983; Hymes 1980; Kress 1985; Michaels 1981; Scollon & Scollon 1981; Scribner & Cole 1981; Street 1984; Wells 1986).

What was in the mind/brain supported these practices, of course, just as the human body did, as well. But even a person's ability to read could vary across contexts. Young people who could not read at grade level in school can, for example, sometimes read well above grade level when as gamers they are reading technical material about a video game they love.

In the late 1980s, I referred to this work, in which I was myself engaged, as "the New Literacy Studies," "NLS" for short (Gee 1989), because I believed that the work shared some common themes and was converging on a new interdisciplinary field of study. The people I included under this label did not necessarily see themselves at the time as being in the same "movement."

Brian Street, one of the earliest and leading scholars in the NLS, has since done more than anyone to institutionalize the

NLS and get it recognized as a consistent approach to literacy studies (Street 1997, 2003, 2005). I myself always viewed the NLS as a loose aggregation of people inspired by related work, work often in different disciplines. It was a complex network.

The NLS stressed the plurality of literacy in terms of different socially and culturally defined practices connected to print (different "literacies"). Eventually people applied an NLS-like perspective to practices involving technologies other than print (such as digital technologies), to so-called "digital literacies." We will discuss digital media in Chapter 4.

There is yet another wrinkle to the story. In the mid-1990s a group of scholars from the United States, Australia, England, and South Africa met several times, calling themselves "the New London Group" (because their first meeting was in New London, New Hampshire, in the United States). The New London Group (1996; Cope & Kalantzis 1999) introduced the term "multiliteracies" and stressed the multiplicity of "literacies" in terms of (a) multiple practices using print literacy, (b) practices around multimodal texts that incorporate both images and language and (c) practices around new digital and social media (just really starting at the time).

The New London Group argued, in regard to literacy in all these senses, that people use "signs" (including "grammar") to produce and "design" their own meanings within communities of practice (Lave & Wenger 1991). They do not just "follow rules." They actively invent the resources necessary for the meanings they wish to communicate. This idea anticipated, by some years, the current focus in areas like the New Media Studies (or New Media Literacy Studies) on production and "participant culture" (Jenkins 2006). Furthermore, the New London Group applied this production and participation focus to oral language and print literacy and not to just digital media.

The New London Group saw people as active designers when they produced meanings using oral language, written language, or media. And they called for people to think like active designers when they consumed oral language, written language, or media, a form of critical thinking.

As we have seen, traditionally literacy was looked at as primarily a mental phenomenon, the mental "ability" to read and write. In fact, traditionally all knowledge was viewed as "mental" and literacy itself was just a form of knowledge, namely knowing how to read and write (Snow, Burns, & Griffin 1998). Knowledge was in the head, not out in the world of interactions with other people and various sorts of tools and technologies.

The traditional view saw both literacy and knowledge in terms of mental representations stored in the head ("mind/ brain"). These representations are the way in which information from the world is stored and organized in the mind/brain and in terms of which it is processed or manipulated. Such a perspective leads to focusing on questions about how information gets into the head, how exactly it is organized in the head, and how it gets back out of the head when people need to communicate. And, indeed, these questions have played a central role in much psychological and educational research.

The NLS attacked (or, at times, simply ignored) this mental view of literacy in favor of a historical and sociocultural approach to literacy. Further, the NLS was part of a larger "social turn" in the 1980s in which work in a variety of areas began to look at language, literacy, knowledge, and learning in terms of social and cultural practices (Gee 2000).

Sociocultural viewpoints look at knowledge and learning not in terms of representations in the head, but in terms of *relationships* between individuals (with both minds and bodies) and in terms of physical, social, cultural, and technological environments in and through which individuals think, feel, act, and interact with others (Gee 2004). Sociocultural viewpoints are embodied, contextual, and practice-based. However, this does not mean literacy is always and only "local." Practices can have global scope as they did in Sweden, Greece, and São Tomé and Príncipe.

If we ask, in the spirit of the NLS, "What is literacy?" and "What is it good for?" we immediately hit on a seeming paradox: It will not work to define literacy simply as the ability to write and read, though that seems to be the everyday meaning of the word. To see why this is so we need to run through a rather simple argument (Gee 1989, 2011). The argument has something of the structure of a *reductio ad absurdum*.

Our little argument starts with the assumption that reading (or writing) is central to literacy only to show that this very assumption itself leads to a view of literacy in which reading or writing (ironically, perhaps) plays a less central role than one might have thought. I will sketch the argument as it has to do with reading. There is an obvious analogue of the argument that starts with writing, rather than reading.

Here's the argument: Literacy surely means nothing unless it has something to do with the ability to read. At the level of meaning "read" is a transitive verb, since it always implies that the reader can read *something*. So literacy must have something to do with being able to read something. And this something will always be a text of a certain type. Different types of texts (e.g., newspapers, comic books, law books, physics texts, math books, novels, poems, advertisements, etc.) call for different types of background knowledge, require different skills to be read meaningfully, and are and can be read in different ways.

To go one step further: no one would say anyone could read a given text if he or she did not know what the text meant. But there are many different levels of meaning one can give to or take from any text, many different ways in which any text can be read. You can read a friend's letter as a mere report, an indication of her state of mind, a prognosis of her future actions; you can read a novel as a typification of its period and place, as vicarious experience, as an "art form," as a guide to living, and so on and so forth.

Let me elaborate a bit further on this notion of reading texts in different ways by giving a concrete example. Consider, the following sentences from a little story in which a man named Gregory has wronged his former girlfriend Abigail: "Heartsick and dejected, Abigail turned to Slug with her tale of woe. Slug, feeling compassion for Abigail, sought out Gregory and beat him brutally."

In one study (Gee 2011), some readers (who happened to be African-Americans) claimed that these sentences "say" that Abigail told Slug to beat up Gregory. On the other hand, other readers (who happened not to be African-Americans) claimed that these sentences "say" no such thing. These readers claim, in fact, that the African-Americans have misread the sentences.

The African-Americans responded with remarks like the following: "If you turn to someone with a tale of woe, and, in particular, someone named Slug, you are most certainly asking him to do something in the way of violence and you are most certainly responsible when he's done it." These particular African-Americans (of course, not all African-Americans are the same) read in ways that linked text to experience.

The point is that these different people read these sentences in different ways and think that others have read them in the "wrong" ways. Even if one thinks that the African-Americans (or the others) have read the sentences "incorrectly," the very act of claiming their reading is incorrect admits that there is a way to read the sentences and that we can dispute how (in what way) the sentences ought to be read (and we can ask who determines the "ought" here and why). If we say that the African-Americans have gone too far "beyond" the text (or that other readers who do not read in the same way have not gone "far" enough), we still, then, are conceding that there is an issue of "how far" to go, what counts as a way (or the way) of reading a text.

So far we have concluded that whatever literacy has to do with reading, reading must be spelled out, at the very least, as multiple abilities to "read" texts of certain types in certain ways or to certain levels. There are obviously many abilities here, each of them a type of literacy, one of a set of literacies.

The next stage of the argument asks: How does one acquire the ability to read a certain type of text in a certain way? Here proponents of a sociocultural approach to literacy argue that the literature on the acquisition and development of literacy is clear (Heath 1983; Gee 2004): a way of reading a certain type of text is only acquired, when it is acquired in a "fluent" or "native-like" way, by being embedded (apprenticed) as a member of a social practice wherein people not only read texts of this type in this way, but also talk about such texts in certain ways, hold certain attitudes and values about them, and socially interact over them in certain ways.

Thus, one does not learn to read texts of type X in way Y unless one has had experience in settings where texts of type X are read in way Y. These settings are various sorts of social institutions, like churches, banks, schools, government offices, or social groups with certain sorts of interests, like baseball cards, comic books, chess, politics, novels, movies or what have you.

One has to be socialized into a practice to learn to read texts of type X in way Y, a practice other people have already mastered. Since this is so, we can turn literacy on its head, so to speak, and refer crucially to the social institutions or social groups that have these practices, rather than to literacy ("reading and writing") independent of such practices and their sociocultural and institutional settings. When we do this, something odd happens: the practices of such social groups are never just literacy practices. They also involve ways of talking, interacting, thinking, valuing, and believing.

Worse yet, when we look at the practices of such groups, it is next to impossible to separate the "literacy bits" from the other bits in social practices. Literacy is almost always fully integrated with, interwoven into, constituted part of, the very texture of wider practices that involve talk, interaction, values, and beliefs. You can no more cut the literacy out of the overall social practice, or cut away the non-literacy parts from the literacy parts of the overall practice, than you can subtract the white squares from a chessboard and still have a chessboard.

What the NLS perspective means, then, is that to really understand literacy, you must not stare at literacy head on. You must see reading and writing as but pieces of larger practices that are wholes that cannot be decomposed without loss. It is an irony that the best way to study literacy is not to stare too intently at it, to foreground something else, namely practices in contexts.

We saw in Chapter 1 that some practices can even fairly be said to be literacy practices even when they do not involve reading and writing directly. When we discussed the work on sharing time in Chapter 1, we saw that sharing time in the schools studied appeared to be early literacy training. Children were being helped to talk in some ways like they would later write. Another example of such a practice is a lecture where a professor talks in ways that are linked to written language and that often sound more like a book than a conversation.

At best, we can say that a literacy practice is any social, cultural, or institutional practice that contains written language or is relevant to written language even it contains none. There is a lot more to literacy and a lot more literacy practices than one might have thought when we started with literacy as the simple ability to read and/or write.

People who take a sociocultural approach to literacy believe that the "literacy myth" (Graff 1979, 1987a, b)—the idea that literacy leads inevitably to a long list of "good" things—is a "myth" because literacy in and of itself, abstracted from historical conditions and social practices, has no effects, or, at least, no predictable effects. Rather, what have effects are historically and culturally situated social practices of which reading and writing are only bits, bits that are differently composed and situated in different social practices.

For example, school-based writing and reading leads to different effects than reading and writing embedded in various religious practices (Kapitzke 1995; Scribner & Cole 1981). And, further, there are multiple school-based practices and multiple religious practices, each with multiple effects. Literacy has no effects (though, of course, it may well have certain affordances or tendencies)—indeed, no meaning—apart from particular social and cultural contexts in which it is used, and it has different effects in different contexts (Gee 2004; Graff 1979, 1987a, b; Scollon & Scollon 1981; Scribner & Cole 1981).

But remember, by "contexts" we mean contexts big and small, embedded one in another. The context of the Swedish mother teaching her children literacy was a small context that was part of the larger institutional context of the Swedish church.

Since people in the NLS were not from the same disciplines, some concentrated on larger contexts than others. Different scholars studied literacy in terms of literacy practices at the level of history (Harvey Graff); whole societies (Brian Street); cultural groups like African-Americans and Anglo-Americans (Shirley Brice Heath); social classes (James Paul Gee); schools (Courtney Cazden and Sarah Michaels); local communities (David Barton and Mary Hamilton); jobs and workplaces (Glynda Hull); and in many other sorts of contexts.

Many of the original scholars in the NLS were not from education and were primarily interested in literacy practices out of school. They were interested in showing that literacy was a much wider issue than schools and schooling. They were interested, as well, in exposing all forms of literacy—most certainly including literacy practices in school—as what Street called "ideological," that is, caught up with values, beliefs, power, and politics.

Many people in the NLS or who were influenced by it were actively hostile to psychology and its mental approach to language and literacy. However, ironically, perhaps, at just the time these people were giving up on psychology, psychology was just about to out-grow both behaviorism and "cognitivism."

Cognitivist psychologists studied how the mind/brain processes information and they often took the digital computer as their model or metaphor for the mind/brain (Gee 1992). The mind was seen as "wetware" (analogous to computer hardware) that ran "software" (programs that carried out rule-based computations which constituted "thinking"). Cognitivism showed little interest in the body, in emotions, or in the world in which humans lived beyond being a source of information to be processed (Bergen 2012).

The NLS (correctly, in my view) did not see how this cognitivist perspective on the mind could fully capture the ways in which language and literacy worked in the world, were affected by it, and transformed it in turn. On the cognitivist view, the mind seemed too detached, too asocial, too little tied to context. So the NLS did not talk about mind, but about the world and people interacting in it.

This meant, however, that the NLS could not really explain literacy as both a mental and sociocultural phenomenon and how these two things related to each other. It also meant the NLS had no real theory of the mental aspects of learning with which to compete in the many disputes that raged over schools, schooling, and pedagogies from the 1980s on.

We will see in the next chapter that by the 1990s cognitivism was waning in psychology. It was to be replaced by a family of viewpoints that viewed the mind much more socially than did cognitivism. Though many were reluctant to make the move, there was a possible rapprochement to be made between the NLS and psychology, between society and mind. It is to this issue—the "social mind"—that we turn in the next chapter.

3

THE SOCIAL MIND

Literacy, Learning, and Oral Language

We have seen that literacy is sensitive to, and varies with, social and cultural factors. When the New Literacy Studies turned from individual minds to social practices it faced this sensitivity squarely. At the same time, people who took a sociocultural view of literacy tended to ignore minds and learning in any individual internalized sense.

By the early 1990s, when I wrote a book called *The Social Mind*, it had become clear that psychology was changing. Psychology was beginning to explicate the ways in which minds are themselves social. There was no reason not to make peace between psychology and theories of social practices, between mind and society.

This chapter is devoted to what has been called an "embodied" view of the mind and of learning. Sometimes this viewpoint is called a "situated" view. In this chapter I want to make integral connections among mind, society, language, and literacy. The key to the connections among all these things is human experience in the world. Let us start, then, with some important background information on the development of literacy in school (remember, though, that literacy exists elsewhere in different forms).

If we ask which factors in a child's home life, before coming to school, correlate with that child's success in first grade, one of the most importance factors is what some scholars have called "emergent literacy" (Adams 1994; Teale 1987; Teale & Sulzby 1986). Emergent literacy is composed of all those practices some homes engage in around literacy before a child can read. These practices include playing with letters and sounds, interactive book reading between parent and child, children's pretend readings, children's early efforts at writing often via "invented spelling," and parents' work to connect the books the child has heard to other books and to the world.

Emergent literacy, which takes place for thousands of hours of a child's preschool years in some homes, prepares the child for learning to decode and understand texts in basic ways by first grade. Children with many fewer hours of emergent literacy fare less well in reading in first grade and often learn to read much later. This is a problem because children who are behind in reading in first grade have an over 80 percent chance of being behind in reading and at school in general by eighth grade.

After first grade—when many (but not all) children have already learn to decode print (i.e., to match letters to sounds and vice versa)—what correlates highly with school success thereafter right through high school and college is not emergent literacy, but two other factors: the child's oral vocabulary at five and the number of words a child has heard from an adult before going to school (Dickinson & Neuman 2006; Hart & Risely 1995).

These two factors (oral vocabulary and talk with adults) are undoubtedly connected. If an adult talks a good deal to a small child, the adult soon runs out of directives ("Don't do that!") and talk about the here and now. The adult must go on to talk about his or her experiences in the world, not here and now, but in the past and in preparation for the future. This means that the parent models for the child how to match up words with experience. The parent models how words apply to experiences of different sorts. In the process the child's oral vocabulary, and the nuances with which the child can use that vocabulary, increases.

While all talk that is sustained on a single topic helps young children, the talk of educated parents introduces children to many book-like words they will later see in books and in teacher talk in school. Nearly every child knows vernacular words like "cat," "go," "home," and "ball" before going to school. But more formal words that occur across many academic and public-sphere written texts, words like "account," "probable," "occurrence," "maintain," "emergency," "create," "invent," and so forth, are good early preparation for school and the language of texts school teaches (Beck & McKeown 1991). These are the sorts of words some children, especially from more educated homes, hear in talk a great deal more than do some other children. Note, by the way, the book word vocabulary of English is largely Latinate (based on Latin words), while the more everyday words are Germanic.

For example, consider the remarks below that a mother made to her three-year-old child when they were having a conversation about dinosaurs. The mother ("M" below) and child ("C" below) were looking at a plastic dinosaur, a plastic dinosaur egg, and a little card that contained information about the dinosaur and the egg (from Crowley & Jacobs 2002: 343–345):

C: This looks like this is a egg.

M: Ok well this . . . That's exactly what it is! How did you know?

C: Because it looks like it.

M: That's what it says, see look egg, *egg* . . . Replica of a dinosaur egg. From the oviraptor.

M: Do you have a . . . You have an oviraptor on your game! You know the egg game on your computer? That's what it is, an oviraptor.

M: And that's from the Cretaceous period. And that was a really, really long time ago.

M: And this is . . . the hind claw. What's a hind claw? [pause] A claw from the back leg from a velociraptor. And you know what . . .

C: Hey! Hey! A velociraptor!! I had that one my [inaudible] dinosaur.

M: I know, I know and that was the little one. And remember they have those, remember in your book, it said something about the claws . . .

C: No, I know, they, they . . .

M: Your dinosaur book, what they use them . . .

C: Have so great claws so they can eat and kill . . .

M: They use their claws to cut open their prey, right.

C: Yeah.

Notice the more formal, book-like words the mother uses: exactly, replica, oviraptor, Cretaceous, hind, claw, and prey.

This not only expands the child's early oral vocabulary towards the vocabulary of school. It also affiliates the child with such words and with practices such as answering questions like "How do you know?" and appealing to print as evidence. Such words and practices will be central to school.

So we see that school-based literacy is very sensitive to oral language before school. It is sensitive to emergent literacy, parts of which involve interactive talk with adults. It is sensitive to extended talk with adults and to a child's oral vocabulary before going to school. Literacy is already well in motion before children have ever set foot in a school and on the basis of oral language.

Many children who have not had a great deal of emergent literacy, extended one-on-one talk with adults, and who do not have a large, especially book-like vocabulary, are never given the chance to gain these things in school. They are rushed right to phonics (decoding instruction) and reading tests without having had the necessary preparation for learning these things. The child is cheated out of necessary developmental stages and the necessary foundation of literacy in oral language.

Non-cognitive Skills

We academics exist in silos, loyal only to our own fields. In the first section you have heard what (some) linguists and literacy educators would say about the home-based language-lined factors that make for school success. But there is another unrelated body of literature that has a lot to say about what early home-based factors affect a child's later success in school and society. This literature is part of developmental psychology.

Many years ago, in a famous set of studies now often called "The Marshmallow Studies" (Mischel, Ebbesen, & Raskoff Zeiss 1972; Mischel, Shoda, & Rodriguez 1989; Shoda, Mischel, & Peake 1990), researchers showed that four-year-olds who could delay gratification later succeed much better in school and society than do children who cannot delay gratification. In these studies, a treat the four-year-old liked and wanted was left in front of the child. The experimenter told the child s/he could eat the treat if s/he wanted to. But if the child waited a little while (fifteen minutes), while the experimenter went away, when the experimenter came back the child would get two such treats. The researchers found that children who were able to wait tended to have more successful outcomes later in life (e.g., better SAT scores, more success in school and attaining higher levels of education, a healthier body mass index, among other things).

The four-year-olds who delayed gratification often engaged in interesting strategies. Some distracted themselves by counting out loud or singing songs. In one study, when children were told to imagine the marshmallow as something that was not food (e.g., a cotton puff or white cloud) or to imagine it to have a frame around it like a picture, the children were able to wait longer.

In a later follow-up study it was found that trust played a role (Kidd, Palmeri, & Aslin 2013). Children who did not really trust that the experimenter would get them another marshmallow (because the experimenter had already failed to get them something they were promised) were much less likely to wait. Children who had found the experimenter reliable waited much longer.

The ability to delay gratification is now listed as one of many so-called "non-cognitive skills" (Duckworth, Peterson, Matthews, & Kelly 2007; Tough 2012). There has been a virtual cottage industry of late studying these skills and the ways in which they correlate with later success in school and educational attainment. These are such skills as delayed gratification, persistence past failure, putting up with and even seeking out challenges, and passion and practice to attain goals.

What is interesting about non-cognitive skills (they are sometimes called "character traits," a perhaps unfortunate term) is that they are malleable. While it is very helpful if they are in place by early childhood before school, they can still be taught later, though we have seen that trust is important if teaching is to work. Children (and adults) can learn strategies to improve these skills. Furthermore, these skills correlate better with school success than does IQ.

We will see in Chapter 4 that there are many things young people do out of school that require non-cognitive skills. For example, when young people play difficult video games, they have to learn to persist past failure, to view failure as good for learning, to practice a great deal without immediate awards, and to appreciate challenges. It may well be that some children have non-cognitive skills for things they care about out of school, but not in school (and, perhaps, again the trust issue raises its head here).

How to Put Language and Non-cognitive Skills Together

We have seen that early oral language vocabulary and extended talk with adults correlates with school success. We have also seen that early non-cognitive skills correlate with school success as well. Is there any connection?

There is, perhaps, a connection between these two to be found in the parenting literature. Some scholars distinguish among three large types of parenting (with sub-types within each): Permissive parenting where anything goes; authoritarian parenting where nothing goes and the child does what he or she is told (period); and authoritative parenting where parents set boundaries and rules but negotiate with their children, offer them choices and responsibility, and reason through decisions (Spera 2005). These are obviously, to some extent, stereotypes and there are nuances within each form of parenting.

In general, and when fairly extreme, neither permissive parenting not authoritarian parenting yields good results. Kids with permissive parents do not learn boundaries or delayed gratification. Kids with authoritarian parents do not learn to negotiate with others and make their own choices. Kids with authoritative parents learn boundaries, delayed gratification, responsibility, and how to make good choices. Authoritative parenting is a particular form of nurturing parenting: The child feels protected, but free to explore and even fail within constraints.

We can see that language plays a key role in authoritative parenting: parents negotiate and reason with their children. They listen to their children and talk to them about life, experiences, choices, and consequences. They give their children experiences in the world where they can explore, take acceptable risks, and build their own knowledge and skills. All these things are good for early language development.

At the same time, authoritative parenting necessarily involves non-cognitive skills. Children must learn to delay gratification, take responsibility, explore and face challenges, and persist past failure, as well as earn what they want, but within the safety of constraints, rules, and adult mentoring and authority. Children develop confidence and trust.

The sort of language skills that lead to school success are embedded in highly interactive authoritative parenting. Authority, trust, and individual choice and freedom are established within sustained interactive talk and in mentored interactions involving knowledge building and challenges in the world.

At a wider level, parenting in any society is intended to produce a certain type of child. In the modern world parenting is used not just to nourish children, but also to prepare them more for various positions in the world. It is to this issue that we now turn. The authoritative model can warp into a system more attuned to producing highly empowered children for status in society than in truly nurturing children.

Unequal Childhoods

Annette Lareau, in her book *Unequal Childhoods* (2003), identifies two different models of what it means to raise children in the United States (and other similar countries). One model she calls the "cultivation model." This model is applied mostly, though not exclusively, by middle- and upper-middle-class parents. The other model she calls the "natural growth model." This model is applied mostly, though not exclusively, by parents in the working class or poor parents.

When parents hold the cultivation model of child-rearing, they treat their child like a plant that must be constantly monitored and tended. They talk a good deal to their children, especially about topics that do not just involve the here and now. They use a good deal of "book language" and adult vocabulary around their children, especially in the areas where their children have become "little experts," something these parents encourage.

Even though they are the ultimate authorities in their homes, these parents negotiate with their children so their children get lots of practice in developing arguments and explanations. They arrange, monitor, and facilitate a great number of activities for their children, such as museum trips, travel, camps, lessons (e.g., music), and special out-of-school activities (e.g., ballet). Through these activities, they heavily structure their children's free time (and, yes, sometimes over-stress the children).

They encourage their children to look adults in the eye and to present themselves to others as a confident and knowledge-able person, or at least a person with a right to an opinion. They encourage their children to develop mastery with digital tools, using things like games as a gateway, and help their child relate this mastery to literacy and knowledge development

Even though many of these practices are good for all chil-dren, cultivated children can be, in some cases, too empowered, perhaps even at times obnoxious. They can be over-stressed and in need of more free time to just be children or even child-ish. Regardless of what you think of such parents and their children, however, the evidence is overwhelming that the cul-tivation model is deeply connected to success in school and to aspects of success in society, at least at the level of income and higher-status jobs.

When parents hold the natural growth model, they treat their children like a plant that, with rich enough soil and nutrients, can be left to develop naturally. Such parents love their children and care for them deeply and well. But they do not feel the need to intervene constantly in their children's lives from the earliest years on. Often they cannot intervene as much as more well-off parents because they are busy working and surviving.

They talk less to their children and use less book-like and adult language with them. They tend to use more directives and commands with children and not negotiate with them. They expect their children to be respectful and deferential to adults.

They do not structure all their children's free time and expect them to learn to find things to do with their peers and by themselves. They do not attempt to direct their children's use of digital media (like games) towards school-based skills, an interest in computer software, or higher-order literacy skills.

Children raised with the natural growth model are often hard-working, self-sustaining, and respectful. They are not always comfortable with putting themselves forward or pre-senting themselves as knowledgeable to adults, even when they are. They are not always comfortable with engaging in arguments or explanations, or sharing opinions with adults, especially those they do not know. They have not built up lots of language, experience, and knowledge connected to the myriad of activities children raised with the cultivation model have experienced.

Many children raised with the natural growth model do just fine in school and go on to have significant success in life. But if we look at a statistical level at group trends, such chil-dren tend to do significantly less well in school and in society, at least in regard to income and positions of power and status (which, of course, are not the only or even the most important markers of success). We must acknowledge, too, that the two models we have discussed are really poles of a continuum and there are parenting styles in between.

Despite all the reservations and concessions we can and must make, we have here an equity problem. It is an equity problem that is getting bigger and increasingly involves digital tools, including video games. Children from more privileged homes, raised with the cultivation model, are acquiring a myriad of skills, values, and attitudes that contribute to success in school and to certain sorts of success in society that should be open to everyone. Privileged homes now also use new digital media in highly mentored and powerful ways to further cultivate and accelerate their children.

Many skills these cultivated children acquire are not even on offer in most of our schools, especially the schools many less advantaged children attend. Digital media, especially when coupled with the cultivation model, can widen gaps in knowledge, literacy, and technological skills between rich and poor kids (Neuman 2010; Neuman & Celano 2006). The existing gaps are bad enough. We need to ask ourselves how we can cultivate all our children, in and out of school, while at the same time widening our ideas about success, beyond achievement in school as it is currently defined and purely monetary success later.

In work on non-cognitive skills it has been shown that when children have a lot of stress chemicals in their blood, they do not display non-cognitive skills. They do not flourish. Interestingly, some studies have found high levels of stress chemicals in both poor and rich children.

Poor children live under the stress of want and need and often with overworked, underpaid, and stressed parents. But some rich children believe their parents view them more as investments that must pay off in the future in terms of prestigious colleges and careers than as children worthwhile in their own right (Tough 2012). They are over-scheduled and often dominated by their parents' desires and values rather than their own desires and passions.

In the end the stress of the poor and the rich children is due, in one respect, to the same cause: a society that over-values status and economic success and under-values human difference and development for larger goals than status and money. As a society, we too often assume, or act as if we assume, that people who are not rich, or do not want to be, are "losers." In our race to the top, we do not want to put out a helping hand to others, including those we have stepped on in our hurry for success. In the act we make our society, and even ourselves, less well off in any real sense.

Below we will see another sense of "cultivating" children that is based not on shallow measures of success, but on what it means to have a rich life and to "read the world" in the service of making a better world. But to get there we must turn to what human experience has to do with the mind and with literacy.

Experience and the Mind

In the 1980s one predominant view of the mind was that it was rather like a digital computer. The mind, like a digital computer, was an information processing device. It followed rules, stored generalizations, and logically deduced results. But during the 1980s a competing view was forming. This view— discussed in my book *The Social Mind* (1992)—came in different varieties. The version I will discuss here is often called "embodied cognition" (Barsalou 1999; Bergen 2012; Clark 1997; Gee 2004; Glenberg 1997).

Work on embodied cognition claims that the human mind does not learn by storing generalizations and abstractions. It learns via experience. Human long-term memory is nearly limitless and humans store the experiences they have had in their minds. They then use these experiences to prepare for future action. They do this by consulting their previous experiences to see if any are good guides for how to act and think in the new situation.

However, the mind does not store experience raw. When we have an experience (in the world or via media), we pay attention in certain ways. We foreground certain elements as important, we background other elements as less important, and we ignore some elements altogether. We edit our experiences via our attention (where we focus and don't) and store them in the mind in this edited format. Of course, even if you and I have had a similar experience—even together—you may have edited that experience differently than I did. So you may well use it to plan, think, and act differently than I will.

But the experiences we humans store in our minds are not just like edited videotapes. Our minds are simulation devices. We don't watch a video in our head. We act in our head. In fact, it is as if we have a video game engine in our head (Gee 2013). We can take elements from various experiences we have had (as edited) and combine them to role-play situations and even to create fantasy worlds.

We can role-play to prepare for future action. And you do not even have to play yourself in your mental simulations or games. You can role-play being yourself at a wedding, being one of several different selves you can enact in public, or even role-play being the bride or the minister. You can role-play what might happen if you got too drunk before giving the toast.

Let me give a concrete, though personal example. Say I am asked to give a very short talk—three minutes max. To me these short talks are much tougher than longer talks. There is little room for error. So I prepare these events, often even while I am waiting my turn on a panel, by playing in my head various possible talks, and think about how different types of audience members might respond positively or negatively. Sometimes, when I am in a bad mood, I envision how I could truly "piss off" everyone or certain types of people. I also imagine speaking as a linguist, an educator, a learning scientist, an advocate for a political position, a concerned citizen, an old professor, a gamer, or something else altogether or some combination of these. Then I act, get results, good or bad. I have had a new experience. I add it to my mental store of simulation materials, albeit edited in certain ways based on how I paid attention to the elements of the new experience.

The same thing happens—more or less consciously—as we navigate the world. We act in our heads in goal-based and problem-solving ways. Humans learn best from experience when they have a lucid goal for taking an action whose outcome they care about in the experience. This helps us manage our attentional economy in ways that helpfully guide how to edit, store, and integrate the experience with others in our minds.

When we do not have a goal for an action whose outcome we care about—when nothing is really at stake for us—then we do not learn well from experience. We do not edit it well and do not store it and integrate it with our other knowledge in an effective or deep way.

Saying that humans learn from embodied experiences in the world does not mean that humans cannot form generalizations or abstractions. It means that we humans do this bottom up, so to speak (diSessa 2000). We need to gain a variety of different experiences, store them, find patterns and sub-patterns in them, and gradually find generalizations based on these patterns, though often fluid generalizations open to change as we gain yet more experience.

Learners need to experience something like an equation in physics "too concretely" at first. They need to understand the equation deeply and well in one or a few specific situations. Then they need to gain experiences of more situations where the equation applies. Eventually they see the equation much more generally and know how to apply it correctly across a number of different situations.

This view of the mind has important implications for school. First, people do not learn well or deeply unless they have more than words and texts. They need experiences. Second, they need clear goals towards an action whose outcome they care about. Third, they must be helped to know how to pay attention in the experience, to know what to focus on, what to background, and what to ignore, so they can edit it well and usefully. Fourth, they need lots of experiences of different cases and they need help finding patterns before they truly understand and appreciate generalizations and abstractions. Fifth, they need to be encouraged to seek out new experiences and new challenges to further enrich their abilities to simulate and role-play in their minds and to further test the patterns they have found and the generalizations they have formed.

Language, Experience, and the Mind

When we put this embodied view of the mind together with language we come across an important paradox. When psychology and linguistics meet here, we get a classic chicken-and-egg question.

On the embodied view of the mind words are given meaning not by other words ("definitions"), but by experiences we have stored in our heads. When we hear a word or read a text, we simulate experiences in our head to give the word or text a specific meaning relevant to the context in which it occurred. This I will call "situated meaning" (contextually specific meaning).

For example, consider what your mind does when I say "The coffee spilled, go get a mop" versus "The coffee spilled, go get a broom." Consider too: "The coffee spilled, go stack it again," "Big Coffee is as bad as Big Oil," "Coffee ice-cream is delicious." You feel your mind call up different experiences—different images and actions—in each case. You have given the word "coffee" different situated meanings in each case.

So experience gives meanings to words and texts. But, on the other hand, as Vygotsky (1987) has argued, language regulates or regiments or cuts up experience for us humans. We know what categories are out there in the world because our language has given us labels for them. For some people, there are sofas, settees, and couches out there, for others there are only two of these, for some only one, depending on how many words you have and how many distinctions you label.

The words "heat" and "temperature" are used in different ways by everyday people than they are by chemists. Chemists have a different, more technical language that cuts up the world differently than we do when we are speaking the vernacular as everyday people. The same is true of the words "force" and "work" in everyday life and in physics. In everyday life, if you have strained and sweated to push a car and it has not budged, you have done lots of work, but to physicists you have done none.

So we reach a paradox: Experience gives meaning to language, but language tells us how to cut up (regiment) experience. Which comes first? It is a classic chicken-and-egg question. You need chickens to get eggs but you need eggs to get chickens.

For us humans, experience and language boot-strap each other. Something or someone has to help us to see how language applies to experience so that we can both gain situated meanings from experience and use language to regiment experience in certain ways. Something or someone has to say things like "pay attention to this here," say words at the right time and place ("just in time"), and help us see a specific variety of language as an emerging "theory" of one way of looking at and cutting up the world.

We need parents, teachers, more advanced peers, and social groups and institutions that supply, mentor, monitor, and assess the ways in which leaners marry language and experience. And, in this sense, all learning is some form of language development. We don't go it alone; we can't.

The Social Mind

The mind is a simulation device or even a game engine to form mental simulations from previous experiences. These simulations give meanings to words and texts. Based on claims like these, we come to a surprising conclusion: the mind is social and there really is no yawning gap between the mind and social practices the NLS studied.

We learn from experience. We store our experiences in our heads in an edited fashion. All of us have had different experiences and edited similar experiences differently. So our heads are different, our brains are wired via experience differently. So how can we ever communicate and collaborate when our different experiences are giving words different meanings and guiding us to think, plan, and act in different ways?

Something must ensure that our heads—and, thus, our experiences in the world—are similar enough and edited and used in similar enough ways that we can communicate and collaborate. This "something" is the social and cultural groups and institutions to which we belong. They ensure we have certain sorts of experiences, edit them in certain ways, and use them for planning and action in certain ways. They ensure we have the necessary experiences, edited in the "right" way, so that we acquire the "right" language that regiments experience in the "right" way and that we assign the words of that language the "right" situated meanings in the appropriate contexts. And here "right" means the way in which the social group, culture, or institution does it, based on their history, values, and practices.

The social world furnishes our minds by supplying us well-designed and well-mentored experiences. As long as our experiences have been similar enough—because we have been helped to have such similar experiences—then the mind will take care of itself. The mind will mirror the social world. The mind will be social. Because the mind is based on experience, the real action is, for us humans, out there in the social world and its myriad practices, just as the NLS said.

Now all this does not mean you have to be any sort of "dupe" for your social groups, blindly following their dictates because they have controlled your experiences and, thus, too, your mind. Of course, this can—and too often does—happen. But we can all belong to more than one social group. We can compare and contrast the experiences and languages of these groups, and, in the act, we can form blended, even new, ways to see and act on the world.

The process is always social—rooted in socially mentored and shared experiences. But it does not have to be—and should not be—socially isolating. If your island is too small, swim to another one.

Language and Literacy

There are many different varieties of language. There are regional and ethnic dialects, academic varieties of language, and varieties used by gangs, lawyers, and bankers. We humans continually invent ever new varieties, such as the language of *Yu-Gi-Oh* cards, the language of "theory-crafting" for video games, and the language of robotics. I will call all these varieties of language "social languages" (Gee 2011, 2014). They are all different ways to "talk the talk" of a given group as part and parcel of "walking the walk" (which involves more than language alone).

Any social language helps a group to see the world in certain ways, to cut it up and regiment its categories and processes in certain ways. There are "power ups" in video games and "strikes" in baseball. Sometimes new tools allow us to extend the power of a social language to name new things, such as electrons in physics or genes in biology.

Of course, there are differences here. Power ups and strikes exist only because video games and baseball exist as things we humans made up. They are in the strict sense social constructions. But we humans did not invent electrons and genes, though, nonetheless, we discovered them and named them and placed them into systems of which they are one part. There are other ways to see and name such systems. We had different ways in the past and we may have different ways in the future.

At the same time, as we have seen, words in any social language only have situated meanings based on experiences we have had—images we have seen, actions we have taken—in the world (or via media). When I say to a baseball fan it was a "foul tip," the fan sees the meaning in his or her mind thanks to his or her experiences with the game. The fan does not think it means a bad piece of advice. When physicists talk about the spin of an electron or light as either a wave or particle, they see images (some from their tools and graphs) in the mind (and it has been shown that some of them can even imagine themselves moving as an electron through an electromagnetic field). When I say to a gamer that, in a particular game, you have to "walk back to your body when you die," the gamer does not ask how one can walk without a body, but sees just what I mean.

So social languages regiment experience (tell us how to look at it and what is in it) and that self-same experience gives the social language situated meanings. That was our chicken-and-egg dilemma above. Learning inherently involves having experiences juxtaposed with language (often from a mentor) so that the experience can give the language meaning and the language can give the experience shape and form. Learning is very often a form of social language acquisition. It today often, as we have seen, involves tools that extend the sorts of experiences we can have in the world or create wholly new ones.

All of this is as relevant to written language as to oral language. In order to "talk the talk" of a group—as part of "walking the walk"—people often have to be able to talk in certain ways and write in certain (related) ways. Let us turn to an example.

Below are two sentences which could have been uttered or written (Gee 2014). The first is in vernacular English, the variety of English people speak when they are speaking as everyday people, not as specialists of any sort (and different people have different varieties of the vernacular based on their social and cultural affiliations). The second sentence is one variety of the family of social languages we can call "academic language."

Academic language is a type of specialist social language (there are other specialists than academics).

1. Hornworms sure vary a lot in how well they grow.
2. Hornworm growth exhibits a significant amount of variation.

These two social languages both draw on the grammar of English at large, but they use that grammar differently for different purposes. The first sentence is about hornworms, cute green caterpillars with yellow horns. The second sentence is about hornworm growth, an abstract property of hornworms (much less cute than hornworms).

The first sentence uses dynamic verbs like "grow" and "vary." These name visible changes. The second sentence turns these processes into things named by nouns: "growth" and "variation." As "things" these can now be counted and measured.

The first sentence has the little word "sure" in it. This word expresses emotion and tells us the speaker (or writer) is impressed. The second sentence sounds odd if we try to put this little emotive word in it:

3. Hornworm growth sure exhibits a significant amount of variation.

By the way, if (3) does not sound odd to you, you have not heard and read enough academic language. If it does sound very odd to you, you have probably read and heard too much academic language.

Finally, note that the basis on which the claim in the first sentence is made is the speaker's (or writer's) own opinion based on what he or she has seen of his or her hornworms.

The basis on which the claim in the second sentence is made is the measurement (statistical) standards and tools of an academic discipline, not just the claimer's personal opinion based on looking at hornworms. Indeed, all the hornworms could look pretty much alike and there could still be a statistically significant difference among them, or they could look quite different and there could still be no such statistically significant difference. After all, that is why we use statistics, to find differences that may not be readily apparent.

Both sentences (1) and (2) gain meaning from experience: In the first case from raising hornworms and in the second from participating in experiments (or, in either case, being able to imagine such things).

Both sentences also involve varieties of language (social languages) that regiment experience, in the first case in terms of how we "everyday" people see and feel about the world and in the second case in terms of how a certain group of specialists sees the world (and often hides its feelings in its ways of writing and speaking). In both cases, we have learned to "talk the talk" by being mentored into social groups such as families, communities, classrooms, and disciplines.

Of course, not everyone gets to (or necessarily wants to) talk about hornworms as an everyday person happy to play around with hornworms. And not everyone gets (or necessarily wants) to talk about animals as a specialist and a member of a discipline. They may well feel this takes the fun out of animals and the world. But, alas, whether they feel that way or not, academic language (of different types) eventually becomes the predominant social language of schooling and is a massive barrier to school success for those who resist its "charms."

Academic language is a barrier to school for many children. It is best to get ready for it early through copious talk from adults and interactions over fiction and non-fiction books early in life before school and during school's early years. By the time children hit fourth grade (today, often earlier), they are beginning to see complex academic language and will see ever more of it in ever more complex forms as school goes on through high school and college.

Academic language is what creates the well-studied phenomenon of the "fourth-grade slump" or "the fourth-grade drop-off" (*American Educator* 2003). Many children, especially from less well-off homes, seem to be learning to read and even pass early reading tests. Yet at fourth grade, when they face the complexities of academic language, they cannot read well enough to handle such language. Early on they have concentrated on decoding and literal comprehension, but in the case of more complex language they need good skills at vocabulary building, at using complex grammatical constructions, and at deeper levels of comprehension, inferencing, and understanding arguments.

Specialist Social Languages

Academic varieties of language are one type of specialist social language (remember, the term "academic language" is a cover term for a family of different social languages, ranging from the languages of physics and mathematics through the many languages of the social sciences, to varieties of language associated with the arts and the humanities). There are a good many specialist languages associated with other areas than academics, such as the languages of law, carpentry, gardening, computer programming, video games, and many more (Halliday & Martin 1993; Schleppegrell 2004).

It is often said that the reason so many children fail in school is that academic language is hard and it pays to get ready for it early and come from a home that sets academic language's earliest foundations in talk and interactions around books and knowledge. And, indeed, even many an adult—educated or not—is not really a fan of academic language. It is not the sort of thing most adults want to take to the beach for an enjoyable read.

But, in fact, there is evidence that technical and specialist varieties of language are not hard. What is important is not just getting ready early. What is important is being able to learn them in a development setting where the learner is mentored to marry experience and language in the service of a very real interest, or, better yet, a passion. Consider the two texts below. The first is from a high-school science textbook and the other is the text on a *Yu-Gi-Oh* card:

> The destruction of a land surface by the combined effects of abrasion and removal of weathered material by transporting agents is called erosion . . . The production of rock waste by mechanical processes and chemical changes is called weathering.
>
> (Martin 1990: 93)

Cyber Raider

Card-Type: Effect Monster
Attribute: Dark | **Level:** 4
Type: Machine
ATK: 1400 | **DEF:** 1000
Description: When this card is Summoned: Activate 1 of these effects.

- Target 1 Equip Card equipped to a monster on the field; destroy that target.
- Target 1 Equip Card equipped to a monster on the field; equip that target to this card.

Yu-Gi-Oh is a card game that can be played face to face or via video games. It is quite complex. The game involves choosing decks from thousands of cards, and reading and carrying out instructions in language that seems as arcane and "boring" as academic language. Yet *Yu-Gi-Oh* is played by quite young children. I first saw the card above in an earlier version in a game between two seven-year-olds. By the way the earlier version was even worse:

> When this card is Normal Summoned, Flip Summoned, or Special Summoned successfully, select and activate 1 of the following effects: Select 1 equipped Equip Spell Card and destroy it. Select 1 equipped Equip Spell Card and equip it to this card.

Now, children do not find *Yu-Gi-Oh* language hard or boring. In fact, I told the two seven-year-olds that I was impressed by how well they could understand and talk such complex and arcane language. They told me it was easy. They could not really see it as complex. And, by the way, many a kid has taken *Yu-Gi-Oh* cards or *Dungeons and Dragons* manuals (written at a college level) on vacation for fun reading.

There is no evidence that *Yu-Gi-Oh* is only playable by rich kids. Any kid who wants to play it and has a passion for it seems to be able to learn it. Indeed, some researchers have found that children engaged in such popular culture activities for which they have an affinity can read several years above their school reading level.

Yet, in school, academic language—even as late as high school—seems hard and boring to many students. And the acquisition of such forms of language shows gaps between rich and poor and white and black. Perhaps the real issue is not that some children find academic language obtuse and hard. Perhaps the real question is why and how does school make something hard and uninviting that out of school looks easy and enticing?

The answer to this question should be clear by this point in this chapter. *Yu-Gi-Oh* is learned by kids watching others play games, playing them themselves, getting mentored by older kids, and watching TV shows and movies and reading books that dramatically act out the rules of the game.

Kids often spend lots of time on Internet sites discussing *Yu-Gi-Oh* with each other and even write about it. They regularly experience how each piece of *Yu-Gi-Oh* language corresponds to an action, goal, result, or interactive dialogue in the game. *Yu-Gi-Oh* language constructs the *Yu-Gi-Oh* universe and copious experiences in that universe fill that language with nuanced, deep, and game-centered contextually sensitive meanings.

The language from the science textbook above—the language of geology—is just like *Yu-Gi-Oh* language. It is about a world of experiences, actions, goals, results, and interactive dialogue—a world it helps to create. The words in the text are given meaning not just by definitions or reading other texts. They are given meaning via images, actions, goals, results, and interactive dialogue that scientists experience copiously in the world. Both new players and new scientists get mentored to see how experience gives situated meanings to words in a social language that regulates and regiments that very experience.

The language of any science is the language of a "game," that is, it is the language of the actions and practices and problem solving of the scientist. Without such actions, practices, and problems the language of any science is as good as a game manual with no game. For beginners—whether playing video games or doing science—reading the manual without having been able to play the game is cruel and unusual punishment (unless the child has a version of the "game" at home). That is why gamers read manuals and guides after or during play, not before. If the *Yu-Gi-Oh* company taught the game the way we too often teach science, they would be out of business.

Real learning is doing before reading. Reading to do better. Performance before competence, not competence before performance.

The moral here is this: No form of language is hard or boring for those who love the world and the "game" (practices and problems) the language is about and from which that language gets its meaning. Humans are good at learning social languages under the appropriate conditions, that is, the conditions under which humans learn best in school and out of school.

Big "D" Discourses

One thing I hope this chapter makes clear is that saying (language) and doing (action) are closely related. To play *Yu-Gi-Oh* you have to talk, read, and use *Yu-Gi-Oh* language in the right ways (the ways that allow you to play well and have others see you as a player). But you have to get more than just your language right. You have to do the right things as well (engage in the right actions, responses, and interactions with others). Your language and your actions must match if you want to be recognized as a *Yu-Gi-Oh* player.

However, we need to go further. Saying (language) and doing (action) are also inextricably linked to being (identity). By "being" I mean enacting a recognizable socially significant identity. When you play *Yu-Gi-Oh*, other players "read" your words and deeds in order to judge *who* you are. Are you a good

Yu-Gi-Oh player or not? Are you a real fan or not? Are you a "poser" claiming skills you do not have?

The same is true of scientists. Given what this person says and does (together and in relation to each other), is he or she a professional geologist? Top of the field? A good amateur? An autodidact or professionally trained?

In society people are always making guesses about who we are by how well we talk the talk and walk the walk of identities (ways of being in the world). Identities are the warp and weave of our social geography. They are how we humans map out the social space in society.

A great deal of the social work people do is devoted to trying to get recognized and to recognize others as having some specific socially situated and consequential identity. Such recognition is open to negotiation; it is tension-filled; it is subject to change and cancellation; and in some cases it is more clear-cut than in others. Refusals to recognize—withholding recognition—can be deeply consequential.

Whether it is a five-year-old seeking to get recognized as a "good student" in Ms. Smith's kindergarten class, a young Assistant Professor seeking to get recognized as a "Chomskian linguist," a Los Angeles cop seeking to get recognized as a "tough cop," or a Native-American seeking to get recognized as a "real Indian" (an emic phrase, see Wieder & Pratt 1990a, b), the process is, at a theoretical level, the same.

I have called all of these sorts of identities "Discourses" with a capital "D" ("big 'D' Discourses"), using the capital to distinguish "Discourse" in this sense from "discourse" (with a little "d") which just means instances of language-in-use (Gee 1989, 1992, 2011, 2014). Socially significant identities do not belong to us as individuals alone. They belong, as well, to the groups of people and institutions that create the conditions for their recognition. Thus, we need a term for them that goes beyond individuals.

Big D Discourses are ways of using language, acting, inter- acting, valuing, dressing, thinking, believing, and feeling (or dis- playing these), as well as ways of interacting with various objects, tools, artifacts, and technologies, in certain sorts of spaces and at certain sorts of times, so as to seek to get recognized as having a specific socially consequential identity. They are a "package" composed of all sorts of stuff, not just language.

Of course, we can recognize people as bidding for and hav- ing social identities that we don't ourselves have or know how to enact (e.g., a neo-Nazi or neo-conservative fundamentalist). And, remember, this is all about recognition, and recognition is a probabilistic, negotiated, changeable thing. Someone can get recognized one way on one occasion and not on another (Wieder & Pratt 1990a, b).

So think of all the "ways with words, deeds, things, thoughts, and feelings" you would have to "pull off" to get recognized in a particular first grade as a "good student" (the issue goes right down to how you hold a pencil!) or "a good beginning reader" (the issue goes right down to what you do with your finger when sounding out words!). Of course, these matters vary with differ- ent schools, classrooms, and communities. A first-grade teacher is creating a Discourse in her classroom (a way of being/doing a first-grade student and the various sub-identities that this involves, like being or not being an "emergent reader" or a "real reader"), similar to other teachers elsewhere, but not identical.

In any Discourse—being a first-grader or a cop in L.A.— there are a number of related sub-Discourses, for example, "good student," "gifted," "special," "poor reader," etc.; "tough cop," "good cop," "veteran cop," "rookie," "good partner," and so forth. Discourses can nest within Discourses. It is hard to know what a "good cop" is if we do not know what a "bad cop" is. And both are versions of a larger Discourse of being a cop.

Often, too, Discourses that are not nested within a bigger one still need each other. We recognize creationists partly because we know how to recognize evolutionary biologists. And creationists define themselves, in part, in contrast to evolutionary biologists. In cities like Los Angeles, cops and gang members "dance" with each other in ways that help them recognize each other in distinctive ways.

Consider again Leona's sharing-time story in Chapter 1. I came to view what was happening to Leona as having to do with socially situated identities and tried to capture this through the idea of Discourses (Gee 1987, 1989, 1990, 1992, 2014). The story is a bit complicated, because it needs to be.

Let's start with the idea of a "primary Discourse." Nearly every human being attains a "primary Discourse" early in life as part and parcel of being socialized into a family of a given type (where, of course, what counts as one's "family" varies across people and cultures). For each of us, there are ways with words, deeds, things, thoughts, and feelings that, as children, we associate with being a "person like us" (like our socializing group). This is our first sense of identity in life. It is the one that carries the most emotional charge for most people.

As we grow up, especially in a pluralistic society, we have to deal with people who come from different primary Discourses than we do. They come from different sorts of families (or other sorts of primary socializing units) than we do. So we need a way to deal with each other as everyday people in everyday encounters. We can call this our "lifeworld" Discourse.

"Lifeworld" is a word that Habermas (1989) uses for the spaces in which we deal with each other as everyday people, not specialists of any sort. These are the spaces where we have common knowledge and "common sense" as members of the same society or some larger group that transcends our "primary kind."

Some people change and adapt their primary Discourse, at certain times and places, to become their lifeworld Discourse. They retain their original primary Discourse more intact when they "go home" ("going home" means different things for different people). Other people lose or even disown parts of their primary Discourse in the face of the diversity and tensions they find in the larger public sphere. Such people sometimes feel they can't "go home" again.

The distinction between your primary Discourse and your lifeworld Discourse is the difference between how you act, interact, dress, think, value, and talk and in which environments in order to seek to be recognized as "family" versus how you act, interact, dress, think, value, and talk and in which environments in order to seek to be recognized as a fellow everyday person in a larger public. Think, for example, about how you would act and talk at "home" or with a close friend at a bar as compared to how you would act and talk to a fellow student, worker, or member of the public when you are meeting as everyday people, not in terms of special, more narrow, shared identities (like being fellow linguists or fellow football fanatics).

Perhaps, you will interact with someone who is not an intimate of yours, but shares some properties of yours that you take to be core (e.g., being an African-American, working class, or the same religion, etc.) somewhere in between your primary Discourse and your wider public-sphere lifeworld Discourse. And, of course, if you never "leave home" you may not have, or have not much of, a lifeworld Discourse beyond your primary Discourse. Your lifeworld and your "home base" converge on each other.

When we leave our families and go out into the larger public we also run into public institutions and interest groups connected to what I will call "secondary Discourses." Everyone, as they go through life, picks up a variety of different "secondary Discourses," that is, ways with words, deeds, thoughts, feelings, and things that are connected to various "public" institutions and interest groups beyond the family. These are institutions such as churches, workplaces, government institutions, schools, video gamers, *Yu-Gi-Oh* fans, and fan-fiction writers.

When people act within these secondary Discourses, they are not acting as "everyday" people, but as "specialists" in the sense that they are playing special roles (playing out special identities) as part of the work of these institutions or interest groups. We realize that these institutions and groups share certain characteristic ways with words and ways of acting, interacting, thinking, and valuing, as well as using various sorts of objects, tools, and technologies in certain characteristic sorts of environments. These are the "tribes" or "teams" or "niches" that make up social geography.

Even if I am, just as a "citizen," applying for a passport in a government office, I must know how to deal with the language and ways of this bureaucracy. Denny Taylor (1996) once argued that bureaucratic language and the practices it is associated with can become particularly "toxic literacies" for the poor and disadvantaged.

In the case of secondary Discourses, we are not in the everyday world as everyday people anymore. We are in special worlds where people share more narrowly defined knowledge and practices. You don't start talking *Yu-Gi-Oh* language to strangers on the bus. But such language is crucial to your sense of belonging to the special *Yu-Gi-Oh* "tribe."

Secondary Discourses can include domains like academic disciplines and medicine; interest-driven domains like video gaming or gardening; specialized institutional domains like courts, classrooms, and government bureaucracies; or special value-based domains like religions or political parties. All these cases involve ways with words, deeds, things, and tools that go beyond our home-based Discourses and involve us in dealing with each other as "special" sorts of persons, not just "everyday" people.

A particular woman, for instance, might be recognized as a business woman, a political activist, a feminist, a church member, a National Organization of Women official, a PTA member, and a volunteer Planned Parenthood counselor, and many more, by carrying out performances that are recognizable within and by each of these secondary Discourses. While, again, secondary Discourses involve more than language, most secondary Discourses involve styles of language that deviate more or less from anyone's vernacular style of language, even if this only involves distinctive vocabulary.

Schools are filled with secondary Discourses, ranging from being a (recognizable) first-grade student of a certain type, through being a special education student of a certain type, to being a student of mathematics of a certain type. In each case, and many more, the child must act, interact, think, feel, value, use language, and coordinate him or herself with things, tools, and technologies so as to get recognized as having a given identity (e.g., being "special" or "gifted"; being "good" or "poor" as a math student) or, at least, is institutionally positioned to be expected to do so.

Through the home-based practices of some parents, school-based secondary Discourses sometimes come to resonate with some children's primary Discourses. Some children come from homes where early versions of school-based practices and their concomitant identities get mixed in with the child's early socialization into his or her primary Discourse. For example, some parents ask their children at dinner to report on what happened that day and they scaffold the child to do so in the sort of concise, linear, and explicit language we associate with school-based literate talk and with many forms of expository school-based writing (Ochs, Taylor, Rudolph, & Smith 1992). This is obviously a practice which resonates with the sorts of school sharing-time events that Sarah Michaels studied.

This dinner-time "report" is an odd hybrid that (purposely) is meant to bridge the gap between home and school. That is why I say that a school-based practice is being "mixed into" the home-based primary Discourse (selective bits of it are incorporated into key moments where the child's initial sense of self in life is being built at home in the child's primary socialization). It is as if we, over time, put a little lemon flavoring into our children's comfort food in order to prepare them to accept and like lemons later on in life.

What is important here is not the school-like practices *per se*, in my view. Rather, what is important is that when such families incorporate a myriad of such early versions of school-based practices into the development of their children's primary Discourses, their children come to see the ways with words, deeds, things, thoughts, and feelings associated with such practices as part of their core sense of who they are in the world. "People like us" do things like this even when we are just "being ourselves." Such children, early on in school, recognize school as a place and set of practices compatible with, even linked to or associated with, their primary Discourse.

Other children, like Leona, bring equally rich and complex practices from their primary Discourses to school. Their families also sometimes filter bits and pieces of secondary Discourse practices into the socialization of their children. For example, many African-American homes mix into their home-based socialization of their children selective bits of practices associated with church, as did my home when I was young. Even as a preschool child, I engaged in talk and action at dinner that was connected to religious rituals and this (along with many other things) helped "marry" these practices and their associated attitudes and feelings to my emerging sense of what it meant to be "people like us" (i.e., my primary Discourse). It created a bridge to my more public and institutional identity as a devout Catholic and Catholic school student throughout the early decades of my life.

Leona's primary Discourse (and whatever has been mixed into it to give her a head start on certain secondary Discourses) is not recognized by school and built on as a base for the acquisition of school-based secondary Discourses. In turn, Leona does not bring to school home-based practices that get her recognized readily as an "acceptable" student. There is much less resonance, in both directions, between her primary Discourse and school-based secondary Discourses as these are instantiated at the outset of schooling. While we have studied these sorts of issues a great deal in terms of "race" (an obsession in the United States), they have wider applicability in terms of many other identities.

Thus, we can say that some families make their children feel that school is for "people like us." On the other hand, for other children, children like Leona, school makes them, from the outset, feel that school is not really for "people like them." In my own case, this sort of conflict was partially resolved because I went to intensely Catholic schools that recognized, accepted, and built on my non-middle-class, Catholic-themed, primary Discourse.

Talk of Discourse is important because it keys us into two things. First, the real action in society is at the level of identity formation and the connections (or lack of them) made across identities. The real issue is how people get recognized or fail to get recognized, and in what ways.

Second, the problem of recognition exists at both the micro level of the individual (i.e., Leona and her teachers) and the macro level of institutions and social groups. Individual people inhabit Discourses, they act them out. At the same time, most of our Discourses pre-dated our entry into the world. Discourses exist (and change) through history and, in a sense, use us as mouthpieces to talk to each other through time. What is happening is happening simultaneously at the level of individuals and at the level of institutions and social groups and must be analyzed at both levels.

Conclusion

In the end, I have argued that we need to study saying (language), doing (action), and being (identity) together. We need to see literacy (written language) in terms of practices that are always part and parcel of different Discourses, different ways of being in the world. In a Discourse, oral language, written language, and ways of acting, interacting, and using various tools and technologies at the "right" times and places all go together. We cannot study literacy by itself. Once we remove it from its natural home in Discourses and society, we have something akin to the black squares of a chessboard, but we no longer have chess or a chessboard.

Reading and writing are mental phenomena of just the sort that require "tuning" from the outside social and natural world. Without such tuning, the mind is isolated. The mind is tuned by Discourses and their interactions in the world. The mind is social and the real action is out there in the world, though that action is replayed and its elements recombined ("modded") in the game engine that is our mind/brain. It is replayed and recombined in the service of thought, action, and meaning for oral language, written language, and the world.

4

DIGITAL MEDIA

Literacy and Digital Media

We are impressed by the power of digital media like the Internet, Twitter, and video games. While we are well aware of the emerging power of modern technologies, we often miss the power of old ones. Writing has thus far in history been far more powerful than has the Internet, for instance. Writing allowed for the external storage of memory, communication across large stretches of space and time, and the development of many different specialized domains of knowledge and science (since everything no longer had to be memorized).

Print changes human minds by training our brains to do new things (Kean 2014). It gives rise to new practices and changes old ones. It does not so much destroy earlier practices as transform them and change their place in the larger ecology of human meaning making. We still have poetry, handwriting, and memory, but they have been changed by print and their place in the ecology of meaning-making and knowledge-building practices has changed, as well. Homer's poetry did not play the same role in society that Robert Frost's did. Homer's memory was vastly better than mine, but he had access to far less knowledge than I do. Digital media, too, will not replace literacy but will change the ecology of reading and writing practices.

Print changed the nature of trust. People came to place more trust in someone's oral word than in their written word. Whole professions and institutions arose to vet, test, assess, and interpret written documents. The nature of trust is changing yet again under the force of digital and social media. Digital tools allow for new forms of piracy, evidence, signatures, invasion of privacy, and ownership.

Print allowed people to hide their identity or write in terms of fictional identities, something that has gone much further on the Internet. It allowed people to "hear from" (i.e., read) and "speak to" (i.e., write) a great many more people from a much greater variety of places and backgrounds than they ever could have without it. And, again, digital media are contracting our physical world and expanding our social worlds yet further and in yet new ways,

As I have pointed out repeatedly in this book, though, none of these changes wrought by print were inevitable. And they were uneven across time, societies, cultures, and social groups. There were different effects in different places. Nonetheless, print has had certain tendencies or affordances that certain sponsors or catalysts could unleash. And the same must be said for digital media.

All of this raises questions about digital media: What are their connections to oral language? To print? How are they transforming oral and written language and changing their ecologies? What effects in what contexts are digital media having and likely to have? What institutions or groups sponsor or serve as catalysts for digital media to have certain sorts of effects in certain sorts of practices and contexts? How are digital media transforming human talk, text, action, interaction, mind, and memory, and how can they do this?

We do not yet know the answers to these questions. Things are too new and changing too fast to have answers yet. Furthermore, I cannot take up these questions in any full or really deep way here. But I hope to give at least a taste of some of the issues in regard to literacy, language, and learning.

The Matthew Effect

When we ask about any technology, we do not want to ask what it does all by itself, but what it does in the hands of people and society. For example, it does little good to ask whether guns cause violence. They certainly have the capacity to, since they are well built to maim and kill. But what effects guns actually have depends on the hands that hold them and the societies that harbor them. They will have different effects in different hands and in different sorts of societies. So, too, for digital media.

So what we want to study when we study technology is "person(s) with tool(s) in specific practice(s) sponsored by specific sorts of social or cultural group(s) or institution(s)." Alas, in much of our media, we hear questions like: "Is technology X (video games, social media, the Internet) good or bad?" or "Does technology X lead to violence (stalking, bullying)?" Such questions are meaningless.

It is often said that digital media can level the playing field between rich and poor kids, by giving all children powerful tools for learning. But, like books, digital media can have different effects in different practices. For example, in an important paper, Neuman and Celano (2006) show that introducing digital media into libraries can actually widen the literacy and knowledge gaps between rich and poor children. Digital tools for learning do not level the playing field here, because while the tools are the same, the practices in which they become embedded in the libraries are different.

Neuman and Celano put cutting-edge computer-based digital tools for learning into libraries (such things as science games and other digital learning tools). They put these digital tools into libraries in both well-off and poor communities in the hope that these tools would level the playing field for the poorer children, giving them access to learning technologies they did not have at home. And, indeed, they found that kids in both sorts of neighborhoods flocked to the digital media. But to their surprise, the poorer kids got less literacy skills and new knowledge and the richer ones got more.

In the middle-class communities, one or both parents accompanied their child to the library. These parents engaged in certain types of mentoring for their children. They pushed their children to pick material on the computer that was at or somewhat above their reading level. They encouraged and helped their children to relate their digital learning to talk and books. They insisted that the child pick something and stick with it. With their help, their children were exposed to complex language, orally and in writing, and to the concomitant knowledge structures that such language supports.

The poorer children were often not accompanied by their parents. These children tended to pick material below their reading level, which leads to few gains in reading. They often switched from one thing to another on the computer, rather than sustaining effort and persisting past failure in one problem space. They had no mentoring. They were not helped to connect the digital media to talk, text, and the world.

Over time the differences in the middle-class and poor children's practices at the library actually widened the literacy and knowledge gaps between the richer and poorer kids. This is not to say that the poorer children were not doing things with the digital media at the library that had positive outcomes somewhere in their lives. It is to say that the digital media at the library was by no means levelling the playing field for richer and poor kids in regard to the sorts of skills and knowledge that school and some parts of society best reward.

Of course, we already knew that interactions and mentoring of certain sorts are crucial in the case of literacy. Just having books does not level the playing field in the case of learning to read and use reading for learning in school. And these interactions and mentoring start at home before school.

It is not books or digital media that are important in and of themselves. It is the practices built around them which, in the case of these libraries, included mentoring interactions with adults. If we conclude that such mentoring interactions are crucial in order to make digital media good for school-based learning and for acquiring skills all children will need for modern society, then we must have the social will to make them so for all children.

If we had such a social will as a society we would not make people work multiple jobs to barely stay above the poverty level. We would ensure that all parents had the time, space, peace, and resources to mentor their children. We would resource poorer children with interactive talk and mentoring, not just books, machines, and media. Yet today we have the highest degree of inequality ever in the United States and across the world. We do not have the social will to supply all children the catalysts that make books and digital media work well for school success and success later in society. We leave it to better-off homes to supply these catalysts for their own children and we leave the poor to fend for themselves and call it "equal opportunity."

Both books and digital media display what has been called the "Matthew Effect" (Adams 1994; Rigney 2010; Stanovich 1986). This term is inspired by the Gospel of St Matthew where it says, "The rich will get richer and the poor will get poorer" (well, it actually says: "For unto every one that hath shall be given, and he shall have abundance: but from him that hath not shall be taken even that which he hath").

Children who get immersed in reading and digital learning with rich interactions and mentoring gain skills and affiliations with literacy and learning for school. These skills and affiliations make them want to read and learn more. With more practice they get yet better and yet more motivated for more practice. It is a virtuous circle.

Children who do not get immersed in reading and digital learning with rich interactions and mentoring learn less and often face frustration. They are less motivated to practice more. They become less affiliated with certain forms of literacy and digital learning. And, thus, they fall further behind and get yet more discouraged and unaffiliated. It is a vicious circle.

Thereby, gaps of all sorts—literacy, learning, skills, and knowledge gaps—get bigger and bigger over time, even if at the start they were small and potentially manageable. Letting what we might call "the Matthew Cycle" go on too long is the worst thing we can do if we want to speak to equity and opportunity. When we let it go on too long, we make what is a solvable problem look all but unsolvable, and, thus, weaken our social will to attempt to solve it. Again, it is matter of social will and social will is a matter of values. Do we really value all children?

Literacy learning and digital learning are both affected by the Matthew Effect and for the same reason. As we saw in Chapter 3, learning is based on well-designed, well-mentored experiences in the world, experiences which give situated meanings to words, images, and actions in talk and texts, on screens, and in the world. In regard to what counts in school, we allow some children to get more, deeper, and better-designed and mentored interactions and experiences in the world than others. We thereby create gaps, not just in literacy, but in language, skills, knowledge, learning, and, in the end, in knowing how to learn to learn (i.e., to be a deliberate learner under one's own steam) in regard to school-based success.

Talk, text, media, and the world all go together, since they recruit the same human comprehension/understanding system built on well-designed, well-mentored experiences of the sort that constitute the social mind. Thus, we need to ensure that the experiences and learning that all children get at home are honored in school. We need to ensure, as well, that all children get the experiences, interactions, mentoring, and tools they need for success in school and society.

New Literacies

Today we have many new digital tools to use in new practices to give and take meaning. Oral and written language enter into these practices in new and complex ways. Some scholars refer to these new tools within their associated practices as "new literacies" (Buckingham 2003; Coiro, Knobel, Lankshear, & Leu 2008; Gee & Hayes 2010, 2011; Lankshear 1997; Lankshear & Knobel 2006, 2007).

They are new literacies in two senses: first, they very often involve new uses of oral or written language melded with other modalities like images, actions, and sounds. Second, they involve new forms of decoding and producing meaning from symbols or representations. For example, a gamer needs to know how to "decode" images and actions (and often, too, words) on a screen into meanings (that lead to decisions and actions). This is a new form of reading. And some gamers learn how to use software (which often now comes with the game) to modify ("mod") and design games. This is a new form of writing.

There has been an immense proliferation of digital practices. Scholars are just discovering how to study such practices and society is not near figuring out their implications, perils, and possibilities. Let me give just two related examples from a much bigger universe of possibilities. These examples will stress that, just as with traditional literacy, we must study digital literacies within practices, not isolated from them.

Example 1: Tabby Lou

Tabby Lou (a screen name) is a sixty-one-year-old single woman living in a rural area of Pennsylvania. In our book, *Women as Gamers* (2010), Elisabeth Hayes and I interviewed Tabby Lou, along with a number of other adult women, about playing the video game *The Sims*.

The Sims is a game where players build families and communities and live out their lives in a virtual world. It is a simulation of life—a "life simulator." The game has a massive community of players who also use various websites to design clothes, furniture, and houses for each other (which they can use in their game play) and to share digital stories about their "Sims" (the people in the families they build in the game).

Unlike many other games, the majority of *Sims* players are girls and women (about 52 percent). *The Sims* was designed by the brilliant game designer Will Wright, comes in many versions now, and is the best-selling game in video game history.

Tabby Lou worked for the U.S. Postal Service and worked her way up, serving fifteen years as a postmaster until she retired in 2003 due to a health condition. Her health problems have made her homebound. In fact, she only leaves her home a couple of times a year.

Tabby Lou's adult daughter bought a copy of *The Sims* when it first was released in 2000. Watching her daughter play, Tabby Lou became interested herself. By the time *The Sims 2* was released, her granddaughters also loved to play the game. Tabby Lou got two computers so the girls could play when they came to her house. At that point Tabby Lou just played the game as part of a three-generation family of *Sims* fans.

One day, one of her granddaughters told Tabby Lou she wanted a purple potty for her Sim children. While you can buy potties for your home in the game's shops, the shops offered no purple ones. The granddaughter asked Tabby Lou whether she could build one for her.

What grandmother would disappoint her grandchild? Tabby Lou decided to build a purple potty for her grand-daughter. At the time, this meant she had to learn to use software like Photoshop to make content and to recolor content that could go into *The Sims*. She had to become a 3-D designer and not just a player. This took lots of effort, effort fueled at this point by her passion for her grandchildren.

But Tabby Lou did not have to go it alone. She found a site on the Internet named *The Sims Resource* (TSI). There she got mentoring and access to a wealth of resources. After lots of effort, she made the purple potty and greatly impressed her granddaughter. But she also, in the process, got hooked on the site, stayed in it, and went on to become a top designer of many other things.

Today, only a few years later, Tabby Lou is an internationally known and respected designer for *The Sims*. At the time we wrote our chapter about her, her creations had been downloaded more than thirteen million times! Tabby Lou is old and infirm, but she's a rock star in her world.

Example 2: Alex

Fan fiction—fiction written by fans of a game, movie, television show, or book—is a massive enterprise today (Black 2008). For example, there are hundreds of thousands of stories written by Harry Potter fans on a variety of websites. And there are a myriad more on other topics written by fans of nearly any media product one could think of. On fan-fiction writing sites, writers gain instruction, mentoring, feedback, and an audience (Black 2005, 2007, 2008; Hellekson & Busse 2006; Jenkins 1992).

Fans writing stories based on *The Sims* is itself a big enterprise. Such *Sims* stories are part of the larger universe of fan fiction, but *Sims* stories are different. In their most basic form, *Sims* stories are created by taking screenshots during *Sims* game play. Players write captions under the screenshots, captions that take the form of a continuous narrative. A "writer" has to produce a multi-modal (words and images) "text" using digital tools (the game, graphic-design tools, and sites for posting, reviewing, and critiquing stories).

The Sims Writers' Hangout (SWH) (http://similik.proboards. com/) is where we discovered Alex (born in 1993, Alex is a multi-ethnic girl). Her most recent series, *Lincoln Heights*, is a vampire romance inspired by the famous *Twilight* novels (and now movies). Alex's stories had their own forum thread that had garnered many pages of comments and 15,046 views in just over a year.

Alex writes her stories for fellow teenagers in an affinity space devoted to *Sims* fan fiction. Here is what one teen has to say about Alex's most famous story, *Lincoln Heights*. It is clear that, for this teen, Alex's writing is helpful in a deep way. (All forum quotes are from the discussion thread on Lincoln Height at *The Sims Writers' Hangout*):

> i LOVELOVELOVE Lincoln Heights. When i read it it always seems to cure my sadness and it has actually helped me deal with alot of depression and shit i've been forced to deal with lately. I can't wait until the next chapter is out . . . HURRY UP, ALEX!
>
>   xo. :]

Alex is on her way to being a star, though she is only a teenager. Alex posts regular updates on her blog and on the SWH thread to keep her fans informed about progress on upcoming chapters. She posts "teasers" prior to uploading complete chapters. Here is one example:

Lincoln Heights 2.6 Teaser

A frustrated sigh escaped my lips and I charged at the bush, deciding to test just how strong I had become. Leaves and twigs littered the ground at my feet as I tore at the bushes. I gave grunts of effort as I pulled as hard as my limbs would allow, my muscles flexing. Various cuts were bleeding on my face and arms as I lashed at the remainder of the shrubs. But just when I thought I had reached a clearing, my sweatshirt caught on a high branch. At first I turned to untangle myself, but gave up not too long after. There was no getting it back now so I wiggled out of the shirt and leaped through the last of the bushes and into the clearing.

When Alex started writing stories on the site, she spelled poorly, her writing was weak, and she came close to plagiarizing the *Twilight* books. Others on the site made it clear to her that posted stories had to be well-written, well-spelled, well-edited, and original. And they mentored her and helped her. She saw models of good work and received encouragement and critical feedback on her own work. She has become adept at graphic design and writing. Indeed, some readers now tell her they like her stories better than the *Twilight* stories.

Consider, for instance, the beginning of *Lincoln Heights*. As the story's description, Alex uses a quote:

Description:
    "You cannot call it love, for your age the heyday in the blood is tame"—William Shakespeare

Then the actual story begins with (remember, each of these sentences has a specially designed image accompanying it):

Devin Collins rolled his dark eyes as his younger sister, Julia, whined about leaving all her little friends in New York.
    "I still don't get why 'we' have to move here when it's Ariel's parents who died!"

> Devin glared at his sister. She was ten: five years younger than himself, but she knew exactly how to piss him off.

Note here how "whined" and "little friends" are, though in the narrator's voice, actually infected by Devin's voice, as it is he that would think of Julia as whining and her friends as "little." This is a form of indirect quotation that is common in novels. The direct quotation "I still don't get why 'we' have to move here when it's Ariel's parents who died!" is not explicitly attributed to the sister, but is clearly understood to be her speaking and, indeed, a representation of her whining. The emphasis on "we" gives the word a stress that sounds like whining.

The introduction of Ariel, a character we do not yet know, starts the story *in media res* (in the middle) and, again, places the narration inside the private knowledge and minds of Devin and his sister. This creates suspense and forces the reader to wonder who Ariel is. This, too, is a technique common in novels. And, again, "piss him off," though not a direct quote, is an indirect quote of Devin's language or thoughts. And, of course, "rolling his dark eyes" is a phrasing meant to capture teenage girl readers at the outset (and it does—girls on the thread say Devin is "theirs" and comment on his attractiveness repeatedly). Alex, indeed, knows her readers very well.

Alex's fans' postings have gotten more and more intense as Alex has continued adding chapters to *Lincoln Heights*. She regularly receives adulation from her readers. She is a celebrity. Like Tabby Lou, Alex does what she does for belonging, contributing to others, and appreciation from others, not for money.

Literacy Kits

Alex posts regular updates on her blog and on the SWH thread to keep her fans informed about progress on upcoming chapters, as well as other things about her life and writing. Consider one of these posts below:

> As u can see I gave my page a little makeover! I've had that oldd one for over a year! Needed a change! As 4 LH 1.3 I've got around thirty slides, working up to my usual 127! Patience is all it takes! I garentee it'll B out B4 Xmas though! ;)
>   <3 A

Language like this gives rise to great consternation on the part of some adults. Some of them wonder if such things betoken the death of written language as we know (knew) it. The spelling errors and unedited typos bother some people to no end.

However, we cannot conclude anything about Alex's post and its language unless we embed it in the whole set of practices and the larger activities in which it lives. Alex is engaged in a Discourse. She is enacting the identity of a *Sims* fan-fiction writer of vampire romance. This is an identity her teen readers readily recognize.

This identity involves engaging in actions that compose the larger overall activity of *Sims* fan-fiction writing. This larger activity requires what I will call a "literacy tool-kit." Think of a carpenter. A carpenter carries around a tool-box full of tools, but also carries around a set of skills that allow the carpenter to put these tools to use in order to be a carpenter and do carpentry. So, too, with Alex. She has a tool-kit filled with tools and skills.

Here is just a part of Alex's tool-kit (tools and skills). Note: Many of these are no longer necessary to create stories in *The Sims 3* and *The Sims 4*. Alex originally used the in-game story mode but switched to posting stories on her own website, so I will use the latter as the basis for the took-kit:

Tools

The Sims 2 game (and expansions as needed)

Adobe Photoshop

Personal website (and all it took to create that)

Custom characters (Sims that she designed to represent her characters; this required knowing how to import into Photoshop, use Photoshop editing tools, and save files, then import back into the game)

Custom software designed by players

Custom content designed by other players

Cheats (to remove unwanted in-game features)

Tutorials as needed

Skills

Know how to customize *Sims* characters, settings, actions

Know how to link website (with story) to *Sims* fan sites

Know how to write narrative

Know how to match images with text

Know how to recruit readers (i.e., where to advertise her stories, how to create banners as advertisements, "teasers," etc.)

Know how to edit story images (i.e., shading, cropping, etc.)

Know how to post text and images on website

Know how to create appealing chapter titles

Know how to "stage" images (i.e., how to position characters, remove distracting objects, etc.)

Know how to respond to fans
Know how to work with volunteer editors

I call this a "literacy tool-kit" because the tools and skills are devoted to making ("writing") and taking ("reading") meaning via the use of technologies for encoding and decoding meanings, i.e., language, writing, and digital media.

There are lots of interesting things to say about this tool-kit. First, note such a kit will change as new literacy and digital tools become available. For example, *The Sims 3* and *The Sims 4* made designing pictures easier (more "user-friendly"). This had the effect that fan-fiction writers no long had to master some of the complicated tools and skills Alex did. Making things easier is a "double-edged sword": it makes an activity more widely accessible (more people can do it), but it also lowers some of the skills people need to acquire (people learn less).

Second, note that the post we saw earlier from Alex—the one that bothers some people for its errors and informality—plays a specific role in the ecology of what Alex is doing and who she is being when she is being a *Sims* fan-fiction writer. It is a way to bond with her teen readers and to motivate them to be devoted readers and followers (her fans). Its language is meant to function in these terms and does so very well, indeed.

Note that Alex writes quite differently when she writes her stories. Here she edits them (with others) and they are free of "errors." This is because this form of writing plays a different role in the larger ecology of who Alex is being and what she is doing.

Third, such tool-kits can define for us an alternative notion of "transfer" of learning. As a person moves to new Discourses and new activities, it may be that the tool-kits they demand for mastery contain similar or related tools and skills as earlier

Discourses and activities a person has mastered. We can ask: What is Alex better prepared to do—what Discourses and activities is she better prepared to learn—given the Discourse and associated tool-kit she has already mastered as a *Sims* fan-fiction writer?

Literacy tool-kits are involved in all sorts of activities and Discourses. And, today, they very often blend traditional literacy and digital tools. For example, I am a "birder," that is, someone who likes to go bird watching. I am not a "pro," but it is an identity and activity I value. Here is part of the tool-kit involved:

Tools

Bird books (at home and one I carry in the field)
Binoculars
iPhone
Special clothes (e.g., a vest that holds my bird book)
Bird list (for park or local area I am in).

Skills

Know good sorts of places to go
Know how to navigate in a place (e.g., walk on the border of
    two different habitats)
Know how to look up bird in book in the field
Know how to locate and track birds in the field with binoculars
Know how to identify lots of birds
Know how to look up birds when I need to in the bird book
Know how to use iPhone apps for bird identification and bird
    sounds and calls
Know not to attract birds by playing their calls (a value some
    others do not hold)

Know what features of a bird to keep in mind so I can look up
  information on the bird at home in books and on various sorts
  of media (e.g., the Internet, digital bird guides, videos, etc.)
Know how to use home resources to prepare for trips and to
  reflect on them afterwards.

Note how even this tool-kit combines traditional and digital
literacy and ways of experiences, books, and images giving
meaning to each other. By the way, what bird books, digital
media, and binoculars do is allow birders to "read" birds in different ways than we do as non-birders. Birds and their feath-
ers become named in different ways. They become categorized
into many more categories. And, they become "events" for life
lists and status among birders, among other things.

Of course, birders cannot "write" (produce) birds as physical
animate objects. But they can certainly produce new meanings
for birds. Their newsletters, guides, local lists, and ways of talking
and interacting with each other give whole new nuances, meanings, and import to birds, their activities, and environments.

In the end birders are not just seeing birds (objects in the
world). They are seeing meanings, seeing birds as meaningful
in certain ways. And that is what a literacy tool-kit is all about.

I am suggesting that one way to study old literacies and
new ones, and their combinations, is to ask, for any text, tool,
or practice, how it is situated within a given literacy tool-kit
within the larger social world of Discourses. This goes for
something as old as storytelling or as new as blogs and tweets.

Affinity Spaces

Both Tabby Lou and Alex used Internet sites of certain sorts to
learn and carry out their activities. Today, if you are interested
in video games, citizen science, media production, activism, or

any special topic, you can find geographically distributed, technologically mediated, and fluidly populated social groupings that comprise online communities or interest-driven groups. In earlier work (Gee 2004; Gee & Hayes 2010), I used the term "affinity space" to characterize these forms of social organization. Tabby Lou and Alex were tied to Internet affinity spaces where in one case people designed and shared designs for *The Sims* and in the other case people wrote and read *Sims* fan fiction.

Most such fan or interest sites are completely open; anyone can find them and access their content. Accordingly, one of the easiest and best ways to answer the question of who "belongs" to such a space is simply to say that whoever enters the space (the fan site) is in the group and belongs for however short or long a time they use the site. This sets up a sense of group membership that ranges from short-term lurkers to wholesale aficionados and everything in between.

Affinity spaces do not have to be virtual, although the Internet lends itself extremely well to the creation of such spaces. I will discuss the core features of affinity spaces below and we will see that such spaces are possible—but hard—in the real world alone.

There is a great deal of interest today in learning out of school (Gee 2013; Gee & Hayes 2011). Thanks to new media and digital tools of all sorts, many activities in popular culture are more complex than ever before. For example, card games like *Magic: The Gathering* and *Yu-Gi-Oh* (games that can be played face to face or as video games) involve complex language and thinking. Or, as another example, in a game like *Foldit* players seek to help scientists by finding the optimal folds for different proteins (and recently discovered the optimal fold for a protein that helps cause AIDS, a discovery that had eluded scientists for twenty years).

In many cases today, out of school learning involves affinity spaces in one way or another. Tabby Lou and Alex are just two examples. Today a great many people, young and old, learn from and contribute to affinity spaces. They are often led to these spaces by participating in other media like games, television shows, books, or in various activities in the world. They gain knowledge and skills in a myriad of different areas like writing, arts and media production, health, environmental issues, computer science, citizen science, and many other areas. With enough practice and effort they often become "Pro-Ams," that is, experts without formal credentials, amateurs who are as good as professionals.

Affinity spaces are an out-of-school form of ubiquitous learning. They are spaces where people can count and matter, not for their money or credentials, but for their achievements, effort, and contributions to others. They are places where people can gain status and even fame. They are places where an interest can be fanned into a passion and a passion can lead to grit, mastery, and success.

Different affinity spaces operate by different norms. Indeed, people can choose the norms of interaction they prefer. Some affinity spaces are quite nurturing. Some operate by "tough love." Some can get nasty and even turn toxic. Affinity spaces can flourish, go bad, live or die, like all human activities. At their best, they are a marvelous invention for learning.

Features of Affinity Spaces

In this section, I describe fifteen features that characterize an affinity space with a focus on nurturing affinity spaces. Affinity spaces do not have to have all these features, but they must have most of them:

1. *Affinity spaces are organized around a common endeavor for which at least many people in the space have a passion.*

The common endeavor is primary, not race, class, gender, or disability. Race, class, gender, and disabilities can be used strategically by individuals if and when they choose to use them for their own purposes. While passion defines a nurturing affinity space, not everyone in the space needs to be passionate or fully committed. They must, however, respect the passion that organizes the space; the space will offer them the opportunity, should they wish to take it, to become passionate.

2. *Affinity spaces are usually not segregated by age.* Older people can be beginners; indeed, anyone can begin at any time. Older and younger people judge each other by their passion, desire to learn, and growing skills, and not by their age. In nurturing affinity spaces, the older and more advanced members set a standard of cordial, respectful, and professional behavior that the young readily follow. There are affinity spaces where everyone is similar in age. This was true of the space in which Alex was writing and dealing with her teenage fans. Such sites have a tendency to split when some of the teens come to care more about socialization than skills in the common endeavor. But in the best of these sites, more expert peers serve the role of social leaders helping to maintain norms and standards.

3. *Newbies, masters, and everyone else share a common space.* Affinity spaces do not segregate newcomers ("newbies") from masters. The whole continuum of people from the new to the experienced, from the unskilled to the highly skilled, from the slightly interested to the addicted, and everything in between, is accommodated in the same space. Different people can pursue different goals within the space, based on their own choices, purposes, and

identities. They can mingle with others as they wish, learning from them when and where they choose, They can even "lurk" on—view but not contribute to—advanced forums where they may be too unskilled to do anything but listen in on the experts.

4. *Everyone can, if they wish, produce and not just consume.* People who frequent a *Sims* affinity space often go there to consume, that is, to get content other fans have created, and that is fine. But the space is organized to allow and encourage anyone to learn to build and design. Tools, tutorials, and mentorship are widely offered. In an affinity space, people are encouraged (but not forced) to produce and not just to consume; to participate and not just to be a spectator. Most affinity spaces set high standards for the quality of production. There is rarely "social promotion" or lowered expectations. Indeed, as in other groups of experts (Bereiter & Scardamalia 1993), the standards for production typically rise continuously, as individuals innovate, create new tools, and otherwise push the collective bar for achievement.

5. *Content is transformed by interaction.* The content available in an affinity space (e.g., all the *Sims* houses, rooms, furniture, clothes, challenges, and tutorials) is transformed continuously through people's social interactions. This content is not fixed. People comment on and negotiate over content and, indeed, over standards, norms, and values. Most of what can be found in an affinity space is a product of not just the space's original designers (and certainly not just a company, e.g., the makers of *The Sims*), but of ongoing content production by people in the space.

6. *The development of both specialist and broad, general knowledge are encouraged, and specialist knowledge is pooled.*

Affinity spaces encourage and enable people to gain and spread both specialist knowledge and broad, general knowledge. People can readily develop and display specialized knowledge in one or more areas, for example learning how to make meshes in *The Sims* or how to tweak a game's artificial intelligence (AI). At the same time, the space is designed in ways that enable people to gain broader, less-specialized knowledge about many aspects of the passion which they share with a great many others in the space. Thus, participants can blend their special skills with other people's special skills to collaborate in terms of the larger knowledge they share about their passion and its purposes. Neither isolated experts nor mere generalists are encouraged in regard to people who want to become central to the space (which need not be everyone).

7. *Both individual and distributed knowledge are encouraged.* An affinity space encourages and enables people to gain both individual knowledge (stored in their heads) and the ability to use and contribute to distributed knowledge (Brown, Collins, & Dugid 1989; Hutchins 1995). Distributed knowledge is the collective knowledge accessible through, in this case, the affinity space, and includes knowledge possessed by people, stored in material on the site (or links to other sites), or in mediating devices such as various tools, artifacts, and technologies to which people can connect or "network" their own individual knowledge. Such distributed knowledge allows people to know and do more than they could on their own.

8. *The use of dispersed knowledge is facilitated.* An affinity space encourages and enables people to use dispersed knowledge: knowledge that is not actually on the site itself but can be found at other sites or in other spaces.

For example, in some *Sims* affinity spaces, there are many software tools available on site made by the designers of *The Sims*, but there are links to all sorts of other groups, software, and sites that have tools to facilitate building and designing for *The Sims*. When a space provides access to dispersed knowledge, it recognizes the value of local and particular knowledge available in other places and created by other groups, and the necessary limitations of its own knowledge base and resources.

9. *Tacit knowledge is used and honored; explicit knowledge is encouraged.* An affinity space encourages, enables, and honors tacit knowledge: knowledge members have built up in practice, but may not be able to explicate fully in words (Polanyi 1967). For example, designers of *Sims* content typically learn primarily through trial and error, not by memorizing tutorials and manuals. While tutorials (explicit, codified knowledge) are found in abundance in these spaces, designers rely on personal contact, through forums and messaging, to pass on their own craft knowledge and tricks of the trade. Indeed, some spaces foster the expectation that tutorial authors will also be available to answer questions as other designers try to use their guides. At the same time, the affinity space offers ample incentives for people to learn to articulate their tacit knowledge in words (e.g., when they contribute to a forum thread or engage in group discussion about a shared problem), though tacit knowledge can never be fully and totally explicated in words.

10. *There are many different forms and routes to participation.* People can participate in an affinity space in many different ways and at many different levels. People can participate peripherally in some respects and centrally in

others; patterns can change from day to day or across larger stretches of time. Sometimes people lead and mentor and other times they follow and get mentored. In nurturing spaces this variation is wider than in less nurturing spaces.

11. *There are many different routes to status.* An affinity space allows people to achieve status, if they want it (and they may not), in many different ways. Different people can be good at different things or gain repute in a number of different ways. For example, in the *Sims* affinity spaces we've studied, some people are recognized for their skills as content creators, others for their tutorials, and still others for their roles in creating and managing the spaces themselves. Again, in nurturing spaces there is likely to be more variation and more routes to status, as well as more acceptance of people who do not want high status (and the corresponding commitment), than in less nurturing spaces.

12. *Leadership is porous and leaders are resources.* Affinity spaces do not have "bosses." They do have various sorts of leaders, though the boundary between leader and follower is often porous, since people can lead in some situations and follow in others. Leaders in an affinity space, when they are leading, are designers, mentors, resourcers, and enablers of other people's participation and learning. They do not and cannot order people around or create rigid, unchanging, and impregnable hierarchies. Obviously there are degrees of flexibility in leadership, and while nurturing spaces foster respect for experts and those with more advanced skills, they tend towards less hierarchy.

13. *Roles are reciprocal.* In an affinity space, people sometimes lead, sometimes follow, sometimes mentor, sometimes get mentored, sometimes teach, sometimes learn, sometimes ask questions, sometimes answer them, sometimes encourage,

and sometimes get encouraged. In nurturing spaces, even the highest experts view themselves as always having more to learn, as members of a common endeavor, and not in it only for themselves. They want others to become experts, too. There is, as some of our interviewees reported, a desire to "give back" to others in the space.

14. *A view of learning that is individually proactive, but does not exclude help, is encouraged.* Affinity spaces tend to encourage a view of learning where the individual is proactive, self-propelled, engaged with trial and error, and where failure is seen as a path to success. This view of learning does not exclude asking for help, but help from the community is never seen as replacing a person's responsibility for his or her own learning.

15. *People get encouragement from an audience and feedback from peers, though everyone plays both roles at different times.* The norm of a nurturing affinity space is to be supportive and to offer encouragement when someone produces something. This support and encouragement comes from one's "audience," from the people who use or respond to one's production. Indeed, having an audience, let alone a supportive one, is encouraging to most producers. Many *Sims* affinity spaces provide mechanisms for this feedback, such as guest books where people can post messages to content creators. At the same time, producers get critical feedback and help (usually also offered in a supportive way) from other creators whom they consider either their peers or people whom they aspire to be like some day. Who counts as a peer changes as one changes and learns new things. Everyone in an affinity space may be audience for some people and potential peers for

others—again, more so in a nurturing affinity space than in less nurturing ones.

The list above is based on the online *Sims* affinity spaces we have studied (Gee & Hayes 2010). Other affinity spaces have these features as well. It is possible to implement these features in face-to-face groups, but it is likely to be more difficult, due to institutional constraints, pre-existing status differentials, and even geographical boundaries that prevent people with common interests from coming together. A classroom where learners did not all choose to be there and where an authority figure grades everyone else is not an affinity space and cannot be one.

The above features are not easy to achieve, in either nurturing or less nurturing versions, and they can deteriorate over time. Affinity spaces with the positive learning and growth features present in nurturing affinity spaces are miracles of human interaction. We need to know a great deal more about how they are initiated and sustained. We also need to study how such spaces can be designed to support learning in areas we care about as educators and citizens, locally, nationally, and globally.

Games and Learning

So far we have discussed how learning within a Discourse leads to the mastery of a literacy tool-kit. We have seen how out-of-school learning today often takes place in affinity spaces. We have thus far purposely backgrounded digital tools themselves in favor of the settings, practices, activities, and identities in which they are embedded.

Now it is time to place a digital tool in the foreground and see how it can enhance literacy and learning. There are many tools we could have picked here, but we will focus on just one: video games.

One of the worst educational technologies ever invented was the textbook. Evidence is replete that textbooks do not work well (Graesser, Jackson, & McDaniel 2007). Why? Because they are meant to be one-size-fits-all, all-purpose solutions to learning. Today, more and more, digital games are being hyped as a new silver bullet in education. People want to teach everything through games, just like some people tried to teach everything through textbooks.

In reality, different tools—tools like oral language, written language, collaboration, video, social media, simulations, games, augmented reality, artificial agents, calculators, multimodal media, graphic representations, and many more—have affordances to do some things well and some things less well, poorly, or not at all (Gee 2004). Regardless of affordances, any tool can be used in good or bad ways and is not good and bad all by itself.

Good learning is a system—a complex system—in which minds, bodies, times, places, languages, and tools interact in complex ways (Brown 1994; diSessa 2000; Gee 2013). As educators we want to design and resource such systems. For a given goal or purpose, we want to ask questions like: What are the best ways to organize interaction and collaboration? What are the best uses we can make of different tools? How can we best integrate instruction, interaction, and tools? What are the best problems to focus on and what are the best ways in which to order or sequence them? What are the best ways to give feedback, resource learning, and assess growth and mastery across time? How can we prepare learners for future learning and make them resilient and able to persist beyond failure? How can we teach what they need now and also what they will need in the future? How do learning systems change across time, go bad, give rise to emergent properties, or begin to operate under their own steam?

Every prospective or new teacher soon faces three salient facts about our schools. First, all sorts of people criticize them (far fewer praise them). Second, all sorts of people have different ideas about how to reform them. Third, teachers are among the last people we ask about how schools should be reformed, despite the fact that they are actually there and most reformers are not. These teachers are inundated with new fads and fashions and constant hype about silver bullets that will leave no child behind (Gee 2013).

Today there is a great deal of interest in and even hype about using video games in schools. This includes commercial games like *Civilization*, *The Sims*, *Portal*, or *Minecraft* and educational games like *Dragon Box*, *Quest Atlantis*, *Immune Attack*, or the *i-Civics* games. Video games are billed as a new silver bullet.

Games can indeed create good learning, because they often teach in powerful ways (Gee 2003, 2007; Squire 2011). However, what many people miss in the rush to bring games to school is that the teaching/learning methods good games use can be implemented with or without games (though games are one good tool to be used with others).

In fact, the best game learning, whether in school or out of school, involves a learning system. The game offers guidance, mentoring, smart tools, well-designed and well-organized problems, feedback, and language just-in-time and on demand. But good commercial games are almost always now associated, as well, with interest- and passion-driven learning on the Internet in fan communities, interest-driven groups, or what we called "affinity spaces" above (Gee & Hayes 2010, 2011). Furthermore, gamers engage in all sorts of social interaction within games, while gaming, and around games.

Recent work on learning suggests that human beings do not learn primarily from generalizations and abstractions (diSessa 2000; Gee 2004). They learn from experiences they have had and shared with others. They find patterns in these experiences with the help of good teachers. With enough experience, they can eventually generalize from these patterns to form larger generalizations or principles.

For example, learners who have learned—through simulations or actual experiences in a lab or the world—how Newton's Laws of Motion apply to one situation (e.g., an accelerating car in a race) gain an embodied and situated understanding of those laws. As they gain understanding in more and more situations, they eventually come to see the laws as general and can think about them in abstract ways as applying to a great many situations.

Words in a text or textbook gain their meanings from the experiences people have had, not from definitions in terms of other words. The words in a game manual or strategy guide are about the actions and images in the game; the words in a biology text are about the actions and images in the world as biologists engage with it.

The game and playing is what gives meaning to a game manual or strategy guide. The world of plants, animals, and cells and the actions biologists take in that world is what gives meaning to a biology text. If a student has no experiences (no actions or images) associated with a text, the student cannot understand the text deeply. That is why doing comes before reading. People need experiences before texts make sense, and then they can use texts to learn new things and improve the learning they do in new experiences.

Because learning is based on experience, students do not learn facts ("information") well if we just focus on facts themselves. They learn and retain facts best when they use these facts as tools to engage in actions and solve problems. Teaching that focuses on facts can get paper-and-pencil tests passed, but such learning does not lead to problem solving. Teaching that focuses on problem solving and that uses facts as tools to solve problems leads to both fact retention and problem solving (Shaffer 2007).

However, there is a problem with learning from experience. It can take a lot of time and learners can fail to know what to pay attention to in their experiences. They can be overwhelmed by details and the richness of any experience. The experiences that lead to the best learning are experiences that are well designed and well mentored through good teaching. Such experiences constrain learners' experiences in certain ways and help them manage their attentional economy by knowing what to pay attention to.

And here is where games become one good tool among others: Games are just well-designed experiences in problem solving. Games can inspire us to move beyond silver bullets and textbooks. They can inspire us to see teaching as designing, resourcing, and mentoring learning systems. They can inspire us to use many tools, not one, in well-thought-out and well-integrated ways.

I have argued throughout my work on learning that good games (together with associated affinity spaces) and good learning systems in general have the following properties (e.g., Gee 2003, 2004, 2007, 2013, Gee & Hayes 2010, 2011):

- They focus on well-ordered problems, not facts and information alone.

- They help learners develop crucial non-cognitive skills like being able to accept challenges, to persist past failure, and to engage in lots of deliberate practice through proactive effort and passion (Tough 2012).
- They give learners good tools with which to solve problems, including other players in multiplayer gaming, and facts, maps, graphs, and information when needed.
- They have clear goals but, nonetheless, they encourage learners to rethink their goals from time to time.
- They lower the cost of failure so that learners will explore, take risks, seek alternative solutions, and try new styles of play and learning.
- They put performance before competence, and they put experiences and actions before words and texts. This means learners learn by doing and that they have images and experiences to give deep meaning to the words and texts they read later to resource their play and learning.
- They give copious feedback, and they assess all along the way to ensure that the learner is always well prepared for what comes next.
- They encourage learners and mentor learners to extend and articulate their knowledge (e.g., in affinity spaces) and even produce new knowledge and designs (e.g., by learning to "mod"—modify—games).
- They ensure that at each new level learners face new problems that challenge the routine mastery they have developed through lots of practice on the last level. This has been called "the cycle of expertise" (Bereiter & Scardamalia 1993; Gee 2007). (Note that learning systems, like games, should involve "level design" and how good level design helps learners "level up," that is, reach ever high

levels across time. There is much to be learned from game designers here.)

- They hold everyone to the same high standard, but they allow learners to reach these standards in different ways and in different amounts of time. It does not really matter where or when a learner has started, only where she finishes.

- They deal with transfer as "preparation for future learning." You can see how well learners have learned by seeing how well they do in similar later and harder learning or problems in life.

- They teach learners to collaborate to solve hard problems and allow them to organize some of their own teaching and learning in terms of interests and passions they share with others.

- Gamers have to think like designers to play the games, since they have to figure out how the "rule system" in the game works and how it can be used to accomplish their goals. They can go further and "mod" the game (make new levels or versions) by using the design software by which the game was made. So, too, learners should learn to think like teachers, to teach others, and be able to "mod" the curriculum.

Teaching that accomplishes all of the above factors I will call Teaching as Designing (TAD)—that is, designing good experiences where students solve problems. Good game designers are teachers and good teachers are designers of good learning experiences. Both game designers and good teachers are designing systems with lots of good types of well-integrated interactions and tools, each being used for what it is good at.

Games have a place in teaching, as do a multitude of other tools. But, games are no silver bullet. However, great teachers designing great experiences—with all sorts of good tools at their disposal—can change the world.

Conclusion and Goodbye

First brains arose, in part made by and filled with patterns from experience in the world. Then some creatures became social and began to mentor and monitor experiences so the mind became social.

Then oral (and signed) language came, only to humans in the form we humans know language. Language, in turn, was given meaning by experiences, but it also ordered, regulated, and categorized that experience.

Different varieties of language—different social languages connected to different socially significant identities and activities—eventually arose based on special experiences, special social practices, and special ways of looking at and organizing things in the world. This process really took off with the invention of writing and later print. Social languages, Discourses, identities, and correlated practices proliferated.

New technologies—including now digital ones—gave us humans new ways to make and take meaning with new technologies, now not just letters, but images and simulations as well. They gave us new literacies.

The new and the old melded, mated, and transformed each other, creating a new ecology of meaning making. Ever more new social languages, new symbols systems, new modes and mixtures of meaning making, new identities, and correlated practices proliferated.

The study of literacy is the study of the human urge to supplement oral language with new technologies for making and taking meaning, technologies like art, writing, print, and digital media.

Literacy is not a minor topic, as I once thought it. It is the story of the social mind in search of ever further reaches of meaning making in the service of new forms of life and new worlds. It is the study, as well, of how the ways in which we humans make meaning with technologies create the social and cultural geography of human practices, groups, and institutions, for better and worse.

REFERENCES

Adams, M. J. (1994). *Beginning to read: Learning about print.* Cambridge, MA: MIT Press.

American Educator (2003). *The fourth-grade plunge: The cause. The cure.* Special issue, Spring.

Barsalou, L. W. (1999). Perceptual symbol systems. *Behavioral and Brain Sciences* 22: 57–660.

Barton, D. (1994). *Literacy: An introduction to the ecology of written language.* Oxford: Blackwell.

Barton, D., & Hamilton, M. (1998). *Local literacies: Reading and writing in one community.* London: Routledge.

Barton, P. E., & Coley, R. J. (2010). *The black–white achievement gap: When progress stopped.* Princeton, NJ: Educational Testing Service.

Baugh, J. (1983). *Black street speech: Its history, structure and survival.* Austin, TX: University of Texas Press.

Baugh, J. (1999). *Out of the mouths of slaves: African American language and educational malpractice.* Austin, TX: University of Texas Press.

Bauman, R., & Sherzer, J. (Eds) (1974). *Explorations in the ethnography of speaking.* Cambridge: Cambridge University Press.

Beck, I. L., & McKeown, M. G. (1991). Conditions of vocabulary acquisition. In R. Barr, M. Kamil, P. Mosenthal, & P. D. Pearson (Eds), *Handbook of Reading Research: Volume 2* (pp. 789–814). Hillsdale, NJ: Laurence Erlbaum.

Bereiter, C., & Scardamalia, M. (1993). *Surpassing ourselves: An inquiry into the nature and implications of expertise.* Chicago: Open Court.

Bergen, B. K. (2012). *Louder than words: The new science of how the mind makes meaning.* New York: Basic Books.

Berger, P., Berger, B., & Kellner, H. (1973). *The homeless mind: Moderniza-tion and consciousness*. New York: Random House.

Black, R. W. (2005). Access and affiliation: The literacy and composition practices of English language learners in an online fanfiction commu-nity. *Journal of Adolescent & Adult Literacy* 49: 118–128.

Black, R. W. (2007). Digital design: English language learners and reader feedback in online fanfiction. In M. Knobel & C. Lankshear (Eds), *A new literacies sampler* (pp. 115–136). New York: Peter Lang.

Black, R. W. (2008). *Adolescents and online fan fiction*. New York: Peter Lang.

Brandt, D. (2009). *Literacy and learning: Reflections on writing, reading, and society*. San Francisco, CA: John Wiley.

Brown, A. L. (1994). The advancement of learning. *Educational Researcher* 23: 4–12.

Brown, A. L., Collins, A., & Dugid, P. (1989). Situated cognition and the culture of learning. *Educational Researcher* 18: 32–42.

Buckingham, D. (2003). *Media education: Literacy, learning and contempo-rary culture*. Cambridge: Polity Press.

Cazden, C. (2001). *Classroom discourse: The language of teaching and learn-ing*. Second Edition. Portsmouth, NH: Heinemann.

Chomsky, N. (1957). *Syntactic structures*. The Hague: Mouton.

Chomsky, N. (1986). *Knowledge of language: Its nature, origin, and use*. New York: Praeger.

Clark, A. (1997). *Being there: Putting brain, body, and world together again*. Cambridge, MA: MIT Press.

Coiro, J., Knobel, M., Lankshear, C., & Leu, D. J. (Eds) (2008). *Handbook of research on new literacies*. Philadelphia, PA: Lawrence Erlbaum.

Comrie, B. (1976). *Aspect*. Cambridge: Cambridge University Press.

Cook-Gumperz, J. (Ed.) (1986). *The social construction of literacy*. Cam-bridge: Cambridge University Press.

Cope, B., & Kalantzis, M. (Eds) (1999). *Multiliteracies: Literacy learning and the design of social futures*. London: Routledge.

Crowley, K., & Jacobs, M. (2002). Islands of expertise and the development of family scientific literacy. In G. Leinhardt, K. Crowley, & K. Knutson (Eds), *Learning conversations in museums* (pp. 333–356). Mahwah, NJ: Lawrence Erlbaum.

Dickinson, D. K., & Neuman, S. B. (Eds) (2006). *Handbook of early literacy research: Volume 2*. New York: Guilford Press.

diSessa, A. A. (2000). *Changing minds: Computers, learning, and literacy*. Cambridge, MA: MIT Press.

Donald, J. (1983). How illiteracy became a problem (and literacy stopped being one). *Journal of Education* 165: 35–52.

Duckworth, E. L., Peterson, C., Matthews, M. D., & Kelly, D. R. (2007). Grit: Perseverance and passion for long-term goals. *Journal of Personality and Social Psychology* 92: 1087–1101.

Finnegan, R. (1967). *Limba stories and story-telling*. London: Oxford University Press.

Finnegan, R. (1977). *Oral poetry*. Cambridge: Cambridge University Press.

Finnegan, R. (1988). *Literacy and orality*. Oxford: Basil Blackwell.

Foley, J. M. (1988). *The theory of oral composition*. Bloomington, IN: University of Indiana Press.

Freire, P. (1970). *The pedagogy of the oppressed*. New York: Seabury Press.

Freire, P. (1973). *Education for critical consciousness*. New York: Seabury Press.

Freire, P. (1985). *The politics of education: Culture, power and liberation*. South Hadley, MA: Bergin & Garvey.

Freire P., & Macedo, D. (1987). *Literacy: Reading the word and the world*. Hadley, MA: Bergin & Garvey.

Gee, J. P. (1985). The narrativization of experience in the oral style. *Journal of Education* 167: 9–35.

Gee, J. P. (1989). *Literacy, discourse, and linguistics: Essays by James Paul Gee*, special issue of the *Journal of Education*, 171 (edited by Candace Mitchell).

Gee, J. P. (1992). *The social mind: Language, ideology, and social practice*. New York: Bergin & Garvey.

Gee, J. P. (2000). The New Literacy Studies: From "socially situated" to the work of the social. In D. Barton, M. Hamilton, & R. Ivanic (Eds), *Situated literacies: Reading and writing in context* (pp. 180–196). London: Routledge.

Gee, J. P. (2003). *What video games have to teach us about learning and literacy*. Second Edition, 2007. New York: Palgrave/Macmillan.

Gee, J. P. (2004). *Situated language and learning: A critique of traditional schooling*. London: Routledge.

Gee, J. P. (2007). *Good video games and good learning: Collected essays on video games, learning, and literacy*. Second Edition 2013. New York: Peter Lang.

Gee, J. P. (2011). *Social linguistics and literacies: Ideology in discourses*. Fourth Edition. London: Taylor & Francis.

Gee, J. P. (2013), *The anti-education era: Creating smarter students through digital learning*. New York: Palgrave/Macmillan.

Gee, J. P. (2014). *An introduction to discourse analysis: Theory and method*. Fourth Edition. London: Routledge.

Gee, J. P., & Hayes, E. R. (2010). *Women as gamers: The Sims and 21st century learning.* New York: Palgrave/Macmillan.

Gee, J. P., & Hayes, E. R. (2011). *Language and learning in the digital age.* London: Routledge.

Glenberg, A. M. (1997). What is memory for? *Behavioral and Brain Sciences* 20: 1–55.

Goody, J. (1977). *The domestication of the savage mind.* Cambridge: Cambridge University Press.

Goody, J. (1986). *The logic of writing and the organization of society.* Cambridge: Cambridge University Press.

Goody, J., & Watt, I. P. (1963). The consequences of literacy. *Comparative Studies in History and Society* 5: 304–345.

Graesser, A. C., Jackson, G. T., & McDaniel, B. (2007). AutoTutor holds conversations with learners that are responsive to their cognitive and emotional states. *Educational Technology* 47: 19–22.

Graff, H. J. (1979). *The literacy myth: Literacy and social structure in the 19th century city.* New York: Academic Press.

Graff, H. J. (Ed.) (1981a). *Literacy in history: An interdisciplinary research bibliography.* New York: Garland Press.

Graff, H. J. (1981b). *Literacy and social development in the West: A reader.* Cambridge: Cambridge University Press.

Graff, H. J. (1987a). *The labyrinths of literacy: Reflections on literacy past and present.* New York: The Falmer Press.

Graff, H. J. (1987b). *The legacies of literacy: Continuities and contradictions in Western culture and society.* Bloomington: University of Indiana Press.

Gumperz, J. J. (1982a). *Discourse strategies.* Cambridge: Cambridge University Press.

Gumperz, J. J. (Ed.) (1982b). *Language and social identity.* Cambridge: Cambridge University Press.

Habermas, J. (1989). *The structural transformation of the public sphere: An inquiry into a category of bourgeois society.* Cambridge, MA: MIT Press.

Halliday, M. A. K., & Martin, J. R. (1993). *Writing science: Literacy and discursive power.* Pittsburgh: University of Pittsburgh Press.

Hart, T., & Risely, B. (1995). *Meaningful differences in the early experience of young American children.* Baltimore: Brookes.

Havelock, E. (1976). *Preface to Plato.* Cambridge, MA: Harvard University Press.

Heath, S. B. (1982). What no bedtime story means: Narrative skills at home and at school, *Language in Society* 11: 49–76.

Heath, S. B. (1983). *Ways with words: Language, life, and work in communities and classrooms.* Cambridge: Cambridge University Press.

Hellekson, K., & Busse, K. (Eds) (2006). *Fan fiction and fan communities in the age of the internet.* Jefferson, NC: McFarland.

Hutchins, E. (1995). *Cognition in the wild.* Cambridge, MA: MIT Press.

Hymes, D. (1980). *Language in education: Ethnolinguistic essays.* Washington, DC: Center for Applied Linguistics.

Hymes, D. (1981). *"In vain I tried to tell you": Essays in Native American ethnopoetics.* Philadelphia: University of Pennsylvania Press.

Jencks, C., & Phillips, M. (Eds) (1998). *The black–white test score gap.* Washington, DC: Brookings Institution Press.

Jenkins, H. (1992). *Textual poachers: Television fans and participatory culture.* New York: Routledge.

Jenkins, H. (2006). *Convergence culture: Where old and new media collide.* New York: New York University Press.

Johansson, E. (1977). *The history of literacy in Sweden.* Umeaa: Umeaa University Press.

Kapitzke, C. (1995). *Literacy and religion: The textual politics and practice of Seventh-Day Adventism.* Amsterdam: John Benjamins.

Kean, S. (2014). *The tale of the dueling neurosurgeons: And other true stories of trauma, madness, affliction, and recovery that reveal the surprising history of the human brain.* New York: Hachette Books.

Kidd, C., Palmeri, H., & Aslin, R. N. (2013). Rational snacking: Young children's decision-making on the marshmallow task is moderated by beliefs about environmental reliability. *Cognition* 126: 109–114.

Kress, G. (1985). *Linguistic processes in sociocultural practice.* Oxford: Oxford University Press.

Labov, W. (1972). *Language in the inner city: Studies in black English vernacular.* Philadelphia, PA: University of Pennsylvania Press.

Labov, W., & Waletsky, J. (1967). Narrative analysis: Oral versions of personal experience. In J. Helms (Ed.), *Essays on the verbal and visual arts* (pp. 12–44). Seattle: University of Washington Press.

Lankshear, C. (1997). *Changing literacies.* Berkshire, UK: Open University Press.

Lankshear, C., & Knobel, M. (2006). *New literacies.* Second Edition. Berkshire, UK: Open University Press.

Lankshear, C., & Knobel, M. (Eds) (2007). *A new literacies sampler.* New York: Peter Lang.

Lareau, A. (2003). *Unequal childhoods: Class, race, and family life.* Berkeley, CA: University of California Press.

Lave, J., & Wenger, E. (1991). *Situated learning: Legitimate peripheral participation.* New York: Cambridge University Press.

Levine, K. (1986). *The social context of literacy.* London: Routledge.

Lord, A. B. (1960). *The singer of tales*. Cambridge, MA: Harvard University Press.

Martin, J. R. (1990). Literacy in science: Learning to handle text as technology. In F. Christie (Ed.), *Literacy for a changing world* (pp. 79–117). Melbourne: Australian Council for Educational Research.

Michaels, S. (1981). "Sharing time": Children's narrative styles and differential access to literacy. *Language in Society* 10: 423–442.

Michaels, S., & Cazden, C. (1986). Teacher/child collaboration as oral preparation for literacy. In B. Schieffelin (Ed.), *Acquisition of literacy: Ethnographic perspectives* (pp. 132–154). Norwood, NJ: Ablex.

Michaels, S., & Collins, J. (1984). Oral discourse styles: Classroom interaction and the acquisition of literacy. In D. Tannen (Ed.), *Coherence in spoken and written discourse* (pp. 219–244). Norwood, NJ: Ablex.

Michaels, S., & Cook-Gumperz, J. (1979). A study of sharing time with first-grade students: Discourse narratives in the classroom. In *Proceedings of the Fifth Annual Meetings of the Berkeley Linguistics Society* (pp. 647–660). Berkeley, CA: BLS.

Mischel, W., Ebbesen, E. B., & Raskoff Zeiss, A. (1972). Cognitive and attentional mechanisms in delay of gratification. *Journal of Personality and Social Psychology* 21: 204–218.

Mischel, W., Shoda, Y., & Rodriguez, M. L. (1989). Delay of gratification in children. *Science* 244: 933–938.

Mufwene, S. S., Rickford, J. R., Bailey, G., & Baugh, J. (Eds) (1998). *African-American English: Structure, history, and use*. London: Routledge.

Neisser, U. (Ed.) (1998). *The rising curve: Long-term gains in IQ and related measures*. Washington, DC: American Psychological Association.

Neuman, S. B. (2010). Lessons from my mother: Reflections on the National Early Literacy Panel report. *Educational Researcher* 39: 301–304.

Neuman, S. B., & Celano, D. (2006). The knowledge gap: Implications of leveling the playing field for low-income and middle-income children. *Reading Research Quarterly* 41: 176–201.

New London Group (1996). A pedagogy of multiliteracies: Designing social futures, *Harvard Education Review* 66: 60–92.

Ochs, E., Taylor, C., Rudolph, D., & Smith, R. (1992). Storytelling as a theory-building activity. *Discourse Processes* 15: 37–72.

Olson, D. R. (1977). From utterance to text: The bias of language in speech and writing. *Harvard Education Review* 47: 257–281.

Olson, D. R. (1996). *The world on paper: The conceptual and cognitive implications of writing and reading*. Cambridge: Cambridge University Press.

Ong, W., S. J. (1982). *Orality and literacy: The technologizing of the word.* London: Methuen.

Parry, M. (1971). *The making of Homeric verse: The collected papers of Milman Parry.* Oxford: Clarendon Press.

Pattison, R. (1982). *On literacy: The politics of the word from Homer to the age of rock.* Oxford: Oxford University Press.

Pinker, S. (1994). *The language instinct: How the mind creates language.* New York: William Morrow.

Polanyi, M. (1967). *The tacit dimension.* New York: Anchor Books.

Rickford, J. R., & Rickford, R. J. (2000). *Spoken soul: The story of black English.* New York: John Wiley.

Rigney, D. (2010). *The Matthew Effect: How advantage begets further advantage.* New York: Columbia University Press.

Schleppegrell, M. (2004). *Language of schooling: A functional linguistics perspective.* Mahwah, NJ: Lawrence Erlbaum.

Scollon, R., & Scollon, S. W. (1981). *Narrative, literacy, and face in interethnic communication.* Norwood, NJ: Ablex.

Scribner, S., & Cole, M. (1981). *The psychology of literacy.* Cambridge, MA: Harvard University Press.

Shaffer, D. W. (2007). *How computer games help children learn.* New York: Palgrave/Macmillan.

Shaywitz, S. (2005). *Overcoming dyslexia: A new and complete science-based program for reading problems at any level.* New York: Vintage.

Shoda, Y., Mischel, W., & Peake, P. K. (1990). Predicting adolescent cognitive and self-regulatory competencies from preschool delay of gratification: Identifying diagnostic conditions. *Developmental Psychology* 26: 978–986.

Smitherman, G. (1977). *Talkin and testifin: The language of black America.* Boston: Houghton Mifflin.

Snow, C. E., Burns, M. S., & Griffin, P. (Eds) (1998). *Preventing reading difficulties in young children.* Washington, DC: National Academy Press.

Spera, C. (2005). A review of the relationship among parenting practices, parenting styles, and adolescent school achievement. *Educational Psychology Review* 17: 125–146.

Squire, K. (2011). *Video games and learning: Teaching and participatory culture in the digital age.* New York: Teachers College Press.

Stanovich, Keith E. (1986). Matthew Effects in reading: Some consequences of individual differences in the acquisition of literacy. *Reading Research Quarterly* 21: 360–407.

Stanovich, Keith E. (2000). *Progress in understanding reading: Scientific foundations and new frontiers.* New York: Guilford Press.

Steele, C., & Aronson, J. (1998). Stereotype threat and test performance in academically successful African Americans. In C. Jencks & M. Phillips (Eds), *The black–white test score gap* (pp. 401–427). Washington, DC: Brookings Institution Press.

Street, B. (1984). *Literacy in theory and practice*. Cambridge: Cambridge University Press.

Street, B. (1997). The implications of the "New Literacy Studies" for literacy education. *English in Education* 31: 45–59.

Street, B. (2003). What's new in new literacy studies? *Current Issues in Comparative Education* 5: 1–14.

Street, B. (2005). At last: Recent applications of New Literacy Studies in educational contexts. *Research in the Teaching of English* 39: 417–423.

Stucky, S. (1987). *Slave culture: Nationalist theory and the foundations of black America*. Oxford: Oxford University Press.

Taylor, D. (1996). *Toxic literacies: Exposing the injustice of bureaucratic texts*. Portsmouth, NH: Heinemann.

Teale, W. H. (1987), Emergent literacy: Reading and writing development in early childhood. *National Reading Conference Yearbook* 36: 45–74.

Teale, W. H., & Sulzby, E. (1986). *Emergent literacy: Writing and reading*. New York: Praeger.

Tedlock, D. (1983). *The spoken word and the work of interpretation*. Philadelphia: University of Pennsylvania Press.

Tough, P. (2012). *How children succeed: Grit, curiosity, and the hidden power of character*. New York: Mariner Books.

Vygotsky, L. S. (1987). *The Collected Works of L. S. Vygotsky, Vol. 1. Problems of General Psychology. Including the Volume Thinking and Speech*. Edited by R. W. Rieber & A. S. Carton. New York: Plenum.

Wells, G. (1986). *The meaning makers: Children learning language and using language to learn*. Portsmouth, New Hampshire: Heinemann.

Wieder, D. L., & Pratt, S. (1990a). On being a recognizable Indian among Indians. In D. Carbaugh (Ed.), *Cultural communication and intercultural contact* (pp. 45–64). Hillsdale, NJ: Lawrence Erlbaum.

Wieder, D. L., & Pratt, S. (1990b). On the occasioned and situated character of members' questions and answers: Reflections on the question, "Is he or she a real Indian?" In D. Carbaugh (Ed.), *Cultural communication and intercultural contact* (pp. 65–75). Hillsdale, NJ: Lawrence Erlbaum.

INDEX